M000316916

Most entrepreneur... place to grow their businesses and end up feeling overwhelmed, staying small, and never reaching their goals. *Your Most Important Number* is the operations and leadership guide that you were never given. It's one of the most powerful and practical books I've picked up all year and is a must read for entrepreneurs!

—Evan Carmichael
CEO, EvanCarmichael.com

The concept of a Most Important Number and focusing on key Drivers has helped my team grow and perform to get even better results during my one-year sabbatical. We continue to use the methodology within our leadership team to provide an incredible member experience and valuable insights to help develop a strong community within Genius Network. Plus, I've introduced this framework to some of the other organizations I have invested in, and it has accelerated their results and improved team focus.

—Joe Polish
Founder, Genius Network

We started using the MIND Methodology when I first launched HeroMaker, and the process helped us quickly and collaboratively grow as a team to accomplish great things. Keeping our highly talented team focused, communicating, and collaborating on the right things as we scale to accomplish feats that have never been achieved before has empowered me to focus on achieving the vision.

—Gareb Shamus
CEO, HeroMaker Studios; CEO, ACE Comic Con;
Founder, Wizard Entertainment

The MIND Methodology has helped the leadership teams of my most recent startups, GravyStack and HeroMaker Studios, rapidly focus and align on what is most important even in the face of all of the challenges, opportunities, and changes that are happening in the FinTech and Web3 space. I see this framework and process as an insurance policy that fully leverages investment dollars in these organizations to ensure we get the best result by doing the right things in the right order to create the most value. It has empowered us to develop and acquire a team of rockstars in our organizations and accelerated the pace at which we execute. The Most Important Number framework has been a game-changer for us.

—Scott Donnell
Founder, Apex Leadership Co., Hapbee
Technologies, and GravyStack

System Pavers has used the MIND Methodology framework for the last three years and accountability and focus have improved significantly during this period along with our Net Profit. Our leadership team meetings have been more efficient, and we can quickly identify how each team is performing and how individuals are being developed to achieve their MIN.

—Larry Green
Executive Chair and Co-Founder, System Pavers

I wish all business strategy sessions were as focused and productive as the sessions with Lee Benson and his team. Using their MIND Methodology process gets our leadership team in sync and on track for quicker implementation. I appreciate how our team's focus gets clearer with their accountability process. It's a major growth accelerator!

—Chad Willardson
Founder, Pacific Capital; Co-Founder, GravyStack; and 2x Best-Selling Author

YOUR MOST IMPORTANT NUMBER

INCREASE COLLABORATION, ACHIEVE YOUR STRATEGY, AND EXECUTE TO WIN

YOUR MOST IMPORTANT NUMBER

INCREASE COLLABORATION, ACHIEVE YOUR STRATEGY, AND EXECUTE TO WIN

LEE BENSON

ethos
collective

Dedication

This book is dedicated to the thousands of incredible leaders I have worked with who intentionally accelerated the value their organizations created.

And to our team at Execute to Win, I am so excited about our future as we serve incredible companies.

For Special Bonus Content Associated with this
Book Visit:

Bonus.YourMostImportantNumber.com

Contents

Foreword

Jack Welch introduced me to Lee Benson about ten years ago. He wanted me to evaluate his operating methodology. After spending time with Lee, I was deeply impressed by the simplicity of his methodology—what he calls Most Important Number™ and Drivers™ (MIND™). Lee's method resonated with me immediately. It works!

Simplicity wins.

It's transferable, repeatable, and most significantly, it's visible. Many times in business, we try to get smart and tinker with the tools. When we do, we can introduce complexity into the equation. Try scaling complexity. It's never fun, especially in organizations with growing teams. You're in for a treat. Don't let the simplicity pass you by. Instead, latch onto it, and make it your own. When you do, you'll identify your Most Important Number and start aligning your team around that metric.

I look forward to hearing your stories of business breakthroughs.

—Ram Charan
#1 *New York Times* best-selling co-author and director of several corporate boards in the US, India, China, Canada, and Dubai

Note to the Reader: Winning Means Keeping Score

Humans are hardwired to play, compete, and win. No one needs to teach children this. They discover it naturally in the nursery or on the playground.

It's not just kids, though. Many adults enjoy participating in sports. Even more enjoy watching sports.

Although it's ingrained in us from early childhood, playing, competing, and winning never leaves us. It continues through adulthood and shows up on the sports field, in the classroom, and even in the boardroom. The stakes might change, but the game still operates by the same rules.

The score.

The score tells us there are winners and losers. Imagine a Little League season without a championship or an NFL season without a Super Bowl. How boring would that be? The entire sports industry lives and dies based upon this one element.

No score? No, thank you.

Numbers matter to the players and the fans.

Ironically, business is also a game. There are winners and losers, and all center around one thing—numbers. When businesses don't publish their numbers, employees feel a lack of engagement.

Humans crave feedback. We want to know how we're performing. Numbers tell a powerful story.

Every business *has* numbers, but not every business *knows* its numbers. Fewer businesses know their Most Important Number. The good ones do. This isn't what makes them good, but make no mistake, it's what *keeps* them good.

Not all numbers are equal. Some carry little weight, like how many paper towels you stock in the restroom. Other numbers represent a significant component, like profit margin or client turnover.

The key is identifying your Most Important Number. Failure to do so could mean the end of your business.

This book is that tool—the simple method to help you discover your Most Important Number and significantly improve how your team thinks about creating value.

By identifying your Most Important Number and aligning your business around it, incredible changes begin to take place. We've discovered this simple method increases collaboration, equips teams to achieve strategy, and helps them execute to win.

Literally, **your Most Important Number is the clearest factor that determines whether you're winning or losing**. Without it, you're just playing around. In this scenario, top performers leave, morale declines, and customers get left behind.

But the opposite is true. Discover your Most Important Number and align your time, money, and energy around that number, and you'll start winning. Stay focused on your Most Important Number, and you'll keep winning.

I can't wait for you to experience your winning season, and I'm excited to help you on this journey. This is what makes business fun. It's also what helps you and your people win championships and give back to your communities.

—Lee Benson

PS One more thing. In the introduction, I share the brief origin story of how the MIND Methodology™ came to be. If you're not interested in the context, then skip this section and get right into Chapter One. The "fact-finding" readers may appreciate the history. The "give me the details" readers will want to jump into Chapter One. Either way, it's my honor to welcome you to *Your Most Important Number*.

Introduction

Don't (Just) Wish Upon a Star

I started my entrepreneurial journey $600,000 in debt. I bought a small electroplating company for its debt of more than half a million dollars. At the time, there were only three employees, one being me. We had just lost 90 percent of our business. We had no money in the bank and very little in the way of equipment. But we had a good idea.

I told the other two employees I couldn't afford to pay them during the first year, but I would give them stock instead. One said he knew this would work. The other said it would never work but to sign him up anyway because he just wanted to see what would happen. In the first year, we earned $360,000 in sales, and over the next twenty years, we grew to 500 employees and added two additional companies doing business in sixty countries with 2,000 customers.

We were in the aviation aftermarket business, and our mission was to safely reduce aircraft operating costs. We started our journey by offering our customers roughly eight repairs to specific parts on two different helicopter models. Our first brochure listed the repairs we performed and to call Rick, Lee, or John with questions. We created a tremendous amount of value for our clients as we saved them up to 80 percent of new part replacement costs.

At the time we sold the business in 2016 for a nice nine-figure exit, we had approximately 10,000 FAA-approved repairs and hundreds of FAA-approved parts we manufactured in-house. The year prior to selling, we estimated to have saved our customers $200 million over their next best value alternative, which was often having to purchase new parts.

More than Meets the Eye

This might read like a business fairy-tale now, but things are rarely as they appear. Prior to the big pay-day, we had our own less-than-ideal experience.

I remember feeling like the growth of the company was stuck for a couple of years at about $8 million in sales and 150 employees. At the time, I didn't mind working 70-plus hours a week, but I knew there had to be a better way. We would get aligned on what we needed to do to win, and in short order, things would drift. As a result, I spent a lot of time realigning everyone and being frustrated with the decisions that were being made.

I started studying our company's functional leaders to understand why some achieved desired results from their team, and others did not. Based on the knowledge I gained from this experience, we created a Leadership Audit Checklist our leaders affectionately referred to as the "LACL" (pronounced "lackel").

We identified and categorized our leaders by four distinct levels:

1. Frontline Supervisor
2. Manager
3. Senior Manager
4. President

Each level included descriptive leadership behaviors, operating system elements, and foundational readiness elements we rated green, yellow, or red based on the quality of their results. The LACL generated a total percentage score for each leader, and lo and behold, as one would imagine, the leaders with the highest LACL percentages achieved better results than leaders with low scores.

This new awareness caused us to create a surgical-level leadership development program. We posted all leaders' scores with complete transparency so each could review and find opportunities for improvement. In addition to leaders finding their own opportunities for improvement and acting on them, their managers could see exactly where they needed development next in order to create the most value. Within a few months, all scores improved, and we started growing again. This was an amazing lesson in effective leadership development.

The scores for each person were in three categories:

1. **Leadership traits**—How leaders "showed up" and developed others
2. **Management operating system elements**—Designed to hold leaders accountable for doing what they said they would
3. **Foundational readiness areas**—Created to ensure leaders had the capabilities in place to win now and win later

With improved leadership results now driving growth, we worked to ensure every employee had clearly defined goals related to quality, cost, safety, delivery, and culture. Productively demonstrating work to achieve these goals became a measurement of performance as well as a condition of employment.

Twenty percent of our employees loved the process, and 60 percent worked well within our parameters. The other 20 percent, we had to drag along kicking and screaming. At the time, I didn't care because we were beating our competition globally on any core product on which we chose to focus. The most notable benefit was it gave us a systemic and sustainable mechanism to objectively rank all employees on culture and performance. Figure 1a (below) represents the evaluation results of approximately 500 of our employees in 2015.

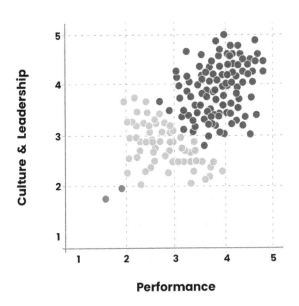

Figure 1a

On the Y-axis, we objectively measured all employees on culture and leadership. On the X-axis, we objectively measured all employees' performance. I loved that even though we were winning globally on all of our core products, there were still lots of opportunities to improve culture and performance.

For additional resources on this topic, including exclusive content and proven tools, visit **Resources. YourMostImportantNumber.com.**

Every Business Runs on a Management Operating System

In 2011 when my colleague and friend Jack Welch (former CEO of General Electric and voted "Manager of the Century") reviewed our operating system, he said it was "the best business management operating system he had ever seen, and had he used it when running General Electric, their results would have been exponentially better."

When I asked Jack why he felt it would have been exponentially better, he said the greatest number of leaders they could ever fully follow, develop, and appropriately position in the organization was the top 500–600 leaders. He felt anything greater tended to become a mostly check-the-box exercise. Jack told me if he had our operating system in place at GE, he could have personally followed, developed, and positioned up to 2,000 leaders.

With Jack's endorsement, in addition to the results we experienced with our clients, I decided to write this book. I wanted to provide access to a proven methodology, tools, and lessons learned for any leader looking to solve the universal leadership challenge of getting teams to consistently create more value over time.

As with most challenges in life, there is no silver bullet to achieve this. The next best strategy to create a culture of winning is creating a management-operating-system-based methodology that works for 80 percent of all teams.

A management operating system (MOS) is generally defined as the set of tools, meetings, behaviors, and general way of doing the work to manage your people and processes to deliver results. As we all know, creating something workable for 80 percent of anything is much easier said than done.

There are several popular management operating systems to choose from, as well as a plethora of organically grown systems. None of these management operating systems are designed around consistently improving the Most Important Number.

As a result, these systems are difficult to sustain because they're based on complexity. As you probably know, it's nearly impossible to scale systems of complexity. Besides, even if you could, it's not fun, rewarding, or stress-free.

In the rare exception they do work, it's because a star team member was driving the process. Likewise, when the star leaves a company for whatever reason, the results simply stop. The results are rarely replicated by another team member because of the level of energy and commitment required to make it work.

Management operating systems shouldn't take a Herculean effort to keep them going. If they do, we are either not doing the systems right or, more likely, trying to force something that doesn't make sense into our organization's culture.

Since I just mentioned culture, let me define it now because it's an important concept within this book. In our context here, I define culture as "what we have agreed to do, and how things get done." As you can imagine, culture and winning go hand in hand. When both of these components are part of an operating system, business becomes truly fun.

A System That Works for Every Business

After our business transformation and then eventual exit, dozens of my friends noticed. Many ran their own businesses and said they wanted to implement the management operating system I developed for my business so they could experience the same amazing results we were getting. Guess what? It only worked for about 5 percent of these CEOs. I believe it took *too much discipline* to consistently drive it over time. In short, it was just too hard for most organizations to sustain.

I've learned what made me wildly successful in my aerospace businesses won't work for most organizations. It is difficult to emulate the results one company gets by trying to replicate what they did.

In my efforts to resolve this, I've studied, tested, and developed a solution to consistently create more value over time and enhance the work of any team in any type of organization. The culmination of this work is what I have named the **M**ost **I**mportant **N**umber and **D**rivers Methodology. We call it the MIND Methodology for short.

MIND Methodology has worked in 100 percent of the teams that truly integrated it. As a result, I've dedicated my life's work to facilitating and implementing the MIND Methodology in organizations.

I created the company Execute to Win (ETW) for this purpose. As it's grown into serving clients around the world, we created customized software to make it much easier to sustain the MIND Methodology over time.

Over the past ten years, we've had the opportunity to work with hundreds of teams and thousands of leaders. In this process, we've studied how teams set goals, developed their leaders, and held people accountable to their vision, mission, and values.

ETW's MIND Methodology and supporting cloud-based software tracks performance and culture, allowing leaders to operate with complete transparency to the inner workings of their organization at any point in time. As a result, the MIND Methodology is a highly collaborative way to do work. It is easy to implement and scale, and it rapidly improves results.

Unexpected Benefits

We've seen how the payoff our clients have experienced from this journey can significantly impact profits, revenue, cash flow, employee alignment/engagement, and more. The biggest payoff I've seen, although completely unexpected, is how the ripple effect of the MIND Methodology has strengthened communities.

Healthy communities take care of their own with little to no outside help needed from the government or anyone else. I saw this time and again within my aerospace business. When employees needed help, team members would organically surround them to get them back on their feet.

Such was the case with Kevin, an employee who injured his spinal cord in an automobile accident on the way to work one day. The injury left him without the use of his legs. Kevin had worked for the company's shipping and receiving department for less than a year. Without being asked to do so, several employees remodeled Kevin's home, so he could have complete access to both floors. When Kevin was able to come back to work, we trained him in a new job, and he is still working in that role today. It was remarkable how the team rallied together to help.

This type of teamwork is contrary to the norm. You've probably seen the research. Approximately two-thirds of all employees dislike their jobs to varying degrees. This unhealthy energy often permeates into the home, workplace, and even their communities.

We are working to change this by offering a solution that energizes and rewards employees at all levels. We have had countless clients who've adopted the MIND Methodology say it has significantly changed their personal lives for the better. This is the positive energy we want to send into the world.

In the process of adopting the MIND Methodology, we've found over 80 percent of employees love and fully engage in their work. This is more than 30 percent higher than "normal" levels of engagement, as reported by Gallup Polls for the past two decades. An elevated level of employee joy and engagement unleashes an amazing flow of positive, productive energy into our employees' communities.

Impacting the larger community creates a much better world for my family, friends, and colleagues. Within this game, using the Mind Methodology, we can all win! And on that positive point, let the games begin.

1

Alignment Begins at the Top

The Senior Leadership Team Sets the Direction

"**A**ttitude reflects leadership, captain."

If you've seen the movie *Remember the Titans*, then you might remember this quote. While this movie is about American high school football, the sentiment remains: A good or bad attitude from the team often comes from the top down.

The context of the dialogue drives the point home. In this scene, two of the football players are blaming each other for their less-than-stellar performance on the field. The score doesn't lie, and clearly, they're not winning. Neither teammate is taking ownership of their role.

The white quarterback blames the black running back for not being a team player. The running back reveals that the white players are not blocking for his black friend. Emotions escalate, and attitudes flare. The scene ends with a pointed truth.

The running back repeats to the quarterback a statement they've both been taught by their coaches: "Attitude reflects leadership."

As leaders of the team, they're the ones who aren't aligned. The whole team is taking their cues from these two leaders. The losing attitude of the team is a direct result of the leaders at the top perpetuating a negative culture.

As you might've guessed, the movie is all about how team unity and alignment at the top can transform an entire team.

Do You Think You're All on the Same Page?

Your MINDset journey begins with some introspective questions around alignment, decision-making, and accountability. We've created the MINDset Assessment™ to make it easy for you and your senior leadership team. Please take the assessment here. Ten simple questions will produce your team's alignment score.

MINDset Assessment

Discover Your Team Alignment Score™

Directions: This MINDset Assessment includes ten simple questions. Please answer each question with your initial gut response openly and honestly. Don't overthink it. At the end of the assessment, you will be provided with your unique Team Alignment Score. If you prefer to take the electronic version, visit **Assessment.YourMostImportantNumber.com**, or scan the QR Code below:

1. Our leadership team is aligned to what is most important to our organization.
    Disagree Strongly | Disagree | Neither Agree nor Disagree | Agree | Agree Strongly
2. Our leadership team is unified and supportive of each other.
    Disagree Strongly | Disagree | Neither Agree nor Disagree | Agree | Agree Strongly

3. Our leadership team numerically measures what is most important.
   Disagree Strongly | Disagree | Neither Agree nor Disagree | Agree | Agree Strongly

4. Our employees are highly engaged in productive, value-creating work.
   Disagree Strongly | Disagree | Neither Agree nor Disagree | Agree | Agree Strongly

5. Our leadership team has an effective process to drive accountability and develop team members to bring more value over time.
   Disagree Strongly | Disagree | Neither Agree nor Disagree | Agree | Agree Strongly

6. Our leadership team makes effective decisions that further our organization.
   Disagree Strongly | Disagree | Neither Agree nor Disagree | Agree | Agree Strongly

7. We have a strong culture of accountability where everyone does what they say and says what they will do.
   Disagree Strongly | Disagree | Neither Agree nor Disagree | Agree | Agree Strongly

8. Our leadership team is aligned on what winning looks like for the next three years.
   Disagree Strongly | Disagree | Neither Agree nor Disagree | Agree | Agree Strongly

9. Our leadership team meetings are efficient and productive, resulting in clear actions with accountable owners and due dates.
   Disagree Strongly | Disagree | Neither Agree nor Disagree | Agree | Agree Strongly

10. Our team does the right work in the right order at the right time to create the most value possible for our customers and stakeholders.
    Disagree Strongly | Disagree | Neither Agree nor Disagree | Agree | Agree Strongly

Team Alignment Score

1. Of your ten questions above, please count how many fit each of the five categories and write that number in the initial blank:

   Disagree Strongly: _____ x (2) = _____
   Disagree: _____ x (4) = _____
   Neither Agree nor Disagree: _____ x (6) = _____
   Agree: _____ x (8) = _____
   Agree Strongly: _____ x (10) = _____

   TOTAL: _____

2. Multiply each number you wrote in the initial blank by the number to the right in parentheses.
3. Total the five sums from the evaluation above to reference the Team Alignment Score Key below.

Team Alignment Score Key

- 0–59: Up until now, our senior leadership team has not recognized the importance of our being aligned. We see a lot of problems related to employee engagement and do not have a culture of accountability. Our senior leadership team hasn't believed our alignment will impact the organization's ability to create value for customers and other stakeholders.

- 60–69: Our senior leadership team has recently begun to recognize the importance of alignment. We recognize our culture and employee engagement may suffer from our lack of alignment. We know there is a better way but have not found a method to get us there.

- 70–79: Sometimes our senior leadership team is aligned, and sometimes they're not. When it comes to alignment on critical decisions or what constitutes creating the most value for our customers and stakeholders, we have different opinions. Sometimes we see opportunities that could cause us to be more aligned, but we're not always sure how to get there.

- 80–89: Generally speaking, our team has figured out how to get on the same page most of the time. The team recognizes there may be opportunities to gain full alignment more quickly. If we do, we can create even more value.

- 90–100: Our team is killing it! We have a clear method of aligning around value creation and making critical decisions. We're unified and committed to creating a clear path to achieve even more success.

Unpacking Your Score

How did you do? Did you struggle to answer some questions? Maybe your score was awesome? Regardless, the smallest tweak can drastically affect the ultimate destination of your team and business.

You've probably heard the story about the airplane that's just one degree off and the unpredictable result. The blogger, 5AM, Joel shares more:

> Imagine an airplane leaving Los Angeles flying directly to Rome, Italy. The flight will take about twelve hours if the plane goes in a direct and straight line. But, if the nose of the airplane is pointed just one degree off course to the south, after twelve hours, the plane will land somewhere in Tunisia, Africa. If there is a one-degree difference to the north, the plane could land in Slovenia or Austria.

We often see businesses "flying" in an unwanted direction simply because their senior leadership team is not aligned in small but significant areas. The goal of any organization is to create the most value it can for its stakeholders and continually increase value over time. To do this, the senior leadership team needs to first agree on what we call the Most Important Number (MIN™), a core foundational component of the MIND Methodology.

As we learned in the Introduction, our Most Important Number is the one number—above all others—reflecting whether the overall business is winning or losing the game. This number measures whether or not you are increasing the value your organization creates over time. The number serves as the North Star of metrics and the foundation for the team to be aligned to what's most important. It also helps you make critical decisions to improve the MIN and hold team members accountable for the work required to arrive at your intended destination. The MIN drives more value-creating behaviors than any other single measure.

Where We're Headed

The rest of this book will help you and your team discover Your Most Important Number. When you do, you'll be able to make every action and decision within your organization to drive improvement. This enhances purpose and motivation, not to mention it increases profit for your company.

While the majority of this book is geared toward for-profit organizations, it has generally been assumed nonprofits are—by design—acting in a socially responsible manner. More than ever before, we have seen a tremendous amount of pressure for both for-profit and nonprofit organizations to behave this way. Today's business pundits espouse *not* making profit the most important metric. This has never made sense to me for two reasons.

First, in my opinion, being socially responsible in terms of improving the communities where an organization engages has always been a common sense, ticket-to-play approach. In every business I founded, I have always worked to improve the respective communities because it not only feels good, but it also generates more profit over time.

With the mindset of improving organizations and their respective communities, it becomes much easier to sustain and grow win-win relationships with customers, suppliers, employees, and communities. It is difficult to sustain profits over the long term if you approach relationships in a win-lose way. The losing party won't choose to hang out with you for very long.

Second, profit as a resource is incredibly beneficial. The more resources we have, the more good things we can do in the world. I believe profit and positive impact on the world are inextricably linked. More profit equals a healthier organization able to weather downturns and create more opportunities for the families depending on the organization for their income and livelihood.

Once you identify your MIN, then your senior leadership team needs to agree that all of your efforts will be in support of improving your MIN. In the for-profit world, the MIN is generally a metric of profit, share price, or cash flow. In the nonprofit world, the MIN will be the most reflective metric to measure the organization's positive impact on its stakeholders. A close second MIN for nonprofit organizations is revenue. We all know that without revenue, nonprofits cannot fund their impact activities. Regardless of the type of organization or industry, establishing an appropriate MIN is the crux of the MIND Methodology.

Equally important to your organization's Most Important Number, let's turn our attention to your products and services to answer the following questions:

- Do you have something scalable based on real-world customer feedback?
- Are those same customers willing to pay for it?

If you answered "yes" to both of these questions, the next most important question for your senior leadership team is the following:

- Are you aligned on the current state of how much value your prospective and existing customers perceive in your products and services?

This last question is foundational for growing the value you create as an organization.

- Does your perception of value in your products and services match what customers are willing to pay for them?

Many senior leadership teams believe their products and services create much more value in the world than customers are willing to pay. Improving the perceived and actual value of your products needs to be a continuous driving force in order to win.

With your senior leadership team aligned on your organization's MIN and able to accurately identify the perceived value of your products and services, the next step is to identify the most impactful work to improve your MIN for the short and long run.

We believe working on the business is a leadership responsibility. Unfortunately, one of the most common things we hear from senior leaders is they are too busy fighting "fires" to do the real work on their organization. As a result, they do very little work focused on getting better results in the future.

So how does a senior leadership team make the jump to work on the business? Start by eating and dreaming.

Eating Versus Dreaming

The best definition of leadership I have ever heard is *eating and dreaming at the same time. Eating* refers to getting great short-term results using what you currently have to work with. *Dreaming* refers to doing things today to get an even better result in the future. In this definition, dreaming is not sitting around thinking about ideas that may be helpful in the future. Rather, dreaming is *doing* things today to get better results in the future.

At the most successful companies I've worked with, senior leaders spend 80 percent or more of their time dreaming.

How much time do you spend eating versus dreaming?

At the most successful companies I've worked with, senior leaders spend 80 percent or more of their time dreaming. There will be days when emergencies come up, and leaders will shift focus to 100 percent eating. But in general, you should pursue an 80 percent dreaming activity state on average.

The reality is most senior leadership teams flip the ideal ratio with 80 percent or more eating and 20 percent or less dreaming. When some senior leadership teams finally make a commitment to achieve a more ideal eating and dreaming ratio, they take twelve to twenty-four months to get there. Don't get frustrated by the time it takes to get there, but rather enjoy the journey. As each month goes by, you'll see positive changes causing your organization to create more value (see Figure 1.1 and Figure 1.2).

**Never stop
eating & dreaming**

You just need to determine the right ratio

Figure 1.1

Figure 1.2

Due to the strategic nature of senior leadership teams, with just a few decisions, some teams can cause much good or much harm. Let me explain. By making a handful of decisions at the top, the team has the ability to create the most value. Conversely, senior leaders also have the potential to significantly harm the organization with a few poor decisions. For these reasons, we believe the senior leadership team's decisions and decision-making framework are the next critical areas to address after identifying the MIN and addressing the four product and services questions.

We all make many decisions each day, yet very few are deemed critical. Senior leadership teams are primarily charged with making a few critical decisions that lead to creating more value for an organization. For the purposes of our work, we define a critical decision as *anything materially impacting your MIN*.

I'm also fairly certain you have work you really like to do and work you really *should* do to create the most value for your organization. It would be perfect if they were one and the same, but this is not normally the case. Your senior leadership team should be doing things to improve your MIN rather than doing low-value work and hoping for the MIN to improve. Ideally, every functional team will have its own agreed-upon MIN, which when improved, will lead to improving the MIN for the next team or teams they support.

By working with thousands of leaders across hundreds of teams, we've discovered the most effective way to improve a team's MIN is to improve the categories of work within the team's control or those they have the ability to significantly influence.

For most teams, there are three to ten categories of work teams should excel at in order to create the most value possible. We call these categories of work *Drivers*. At the senior leadership team level, you should be focusing on Drivers with a holistic, positive impact on your organization. Some examples of Drivers for a senior team can include customer experience, organizational structure, pricing, strategy, leadership development, improving the employee experience, standard operating procedures, and intentional culture.

Senior Leadership Sets the Culture

Another area where senior leadership alignment is critical is the topic of organizational culture.

Many senior leadership teams believe their organization's culture is significantly better than it actually is. This is because there is often a lack of agreement on what the culture should look and feel like. In the rare case

Many senior leadership teams believe their organization's culture is significantly better than it actually is.

there is a consensus, often the senior leadership team fails to connect intentional organizational culture to financial performance.

At the highest levels of leadership in organizations we've worked with, culture is often seen as fluff. If culture is valued, then it's viewed as a cost and sometimes includes such practices as providing snack food in the breakroom or allowing employees to bring their dogs to work. The goal tends to be related to people feeling good. There tends to be little intentional connection between creating a healthy/thriving culture to *driving* financial performance.

Here are some culture questions to consider:

- How do you define culture?
- Does your culture make your organization measurably better?
- Are you able to objectively connect the application of your culture to the financial performance of your organization?

At Execute to Win (ETW) and other businesses I've built, we define culture as "what we agreed to do as a team and how things get done." Actively demonstrating a commitment to all alignment tools (mission, vision, values, purpose) is a critical component of connecting culture to financial results. These alignment tools are the primary decision filters for connecting "what your team agrees to do and how work gets done" to financial results.

Actively demonstrating a commitment to all alignment tools (mission, vision, values, purpose) is a critical component of connecting culture to financial results.

Whatever your team does should be with the intent of making the organization measurably better. Everything else is a waste of time and resources. Efforts to establish and reinforce an intentional culture should pass this test.

Many leaders can recite the mission, vision, and core values, and some even have them printed on the backs of their company identification cards or posted throughout the facility. The goal of organizational culture, however, isn't reciting the mission when called upon. It is *living* an intentionally-based culture to create more value for your organization, your team members, and ultimately, for your customers.

Creating a mission, vision statement, or set of core values is a waste of time if you can't all sink your teeth into them by creating more value and fully connecting them to financial results. Without the connection, it's a futile exercise of looking and feeling good and oftentimes demoralizes employees when the actions of leaders are at odds with the mission, vision, and values created.

You may be wondering, "How do I connect our culture to our financial results?" The first step is to create *intentional and meaningful* alignment tools. Your senior leadership team must agree on how each will create value for your organization before printing them out on the back of everyone's ID card. As a real-world example, I'll share the story of how we created alignment tools in my former business, Able Aerospace.

Case Study: Able Aerospace

Before drafting Able's mission statement, our senior leadership team decided we wanted to tell our customers—in a compelling way—why they should do business with us. At the same time, we wanted to tell every employee why they get a paycheck. Our mission statement needed to reflect what each of us did every day to win, and if we didn't do it, our jobs would be in jeopardy.

We wanted our mission statement to be something we could all rally around to grow faster and more profitably. It took time in thoughtful discussion to draft a mission statement that would do both. We settled on the following:

> "Our mission is to safely reduce aircraft operating costs by providing resourceful component repair, overhaul, and approved replacement parts solutions."

We saved our customers tens of millions of dollars each year over their next best value alternative, which would often be purchasing new parts. Customers I had met for the first time would tell me our mission saved them so much money they were able to buy additional aircraft. Our mission made us nearly recession-proof because, in downtimes, our customers were even more incentivized to safely save on aircraft operating costs. With a powerfully intentional mission in place, it was time to address our next alignment tool, our set of values.

Early on, like most companies, we had a set of values I pulled from a presentation I had attended. The first value at the top of the list was *integrity*. After completing our mission statement exercise, the set no longer felt right, so I tested it. At the time, we had seventy employees.

I asked ten of them how they were applying integrity to their work to make us measurably better, and I got ten crazy answers telling me our original set of values from the presentation I had attended did nothing more than create expensive wallpaper to hang around the facility.

Applying the same methodology we used to create our mission, we created a set of values with the intention to make us measurably better. Our senior leadership team decided we would work to create a condition where, at any point in time, 50 percent or more of our team members would perform, lead, and behave better than the top 10 percent of performers at our strongest, most admired competitors.

To create this set of new values, we surveyed all employees, asking them to write down the *observable behaviors of the best-performing people they had ever worked with on their best days.* We received responses from sixty-eight of the seventy employees surveyed, which included long lists of attributes. We distilled the responses down to six behaviors that have stood the test of time for twenty-one years and counting.

High-performing employees throughout Able Aerospace:

1. Do what they say they will.
2. Are respectful, honest, and straightforward.
3. Treat company resources as their own.
4. Have a personal commitment to the end result.
5. Present and pursue permanent solutions, as opposed to dwelling on problems.
6. Are fully engaged and participate within the team.

Through this exercise, we agreed to formulate desired, observable behaviors and eliminate the subjectivity of interpreting a value. This is because I used to think integrity would mean the same thing to most people, and it simply wasn't the case. We tied the value of integrity with the behavior of "doing what you say you will." Our set of behaviors proved to be a great management tool.

Anytime something didn't go as we wanted, there was at least one of these behaviors not being reflected in the way the entire organization agreed to embody them. We regularly had conversations about applying these behaviors in ways to improve the customer experience (internally and externally) and profitability.

These two powerful experiences led us to create a strong vision statement, a clear set of leadership traits, and a quality policy in the aerospace business. Each went through the same process of ensuring they were designed to create the most value for all of our stakeholders.

Referencing the Able Aerospace Alignment Tools below might bring clarity to your context.

Mission—To safely reduce aircraft operating costs by providing resourceful component repair, overhaul, and approved replacement parts solutions.

Vision—To maximize the return on our core products and be recognized as the industry leader for the services we provide.

Quality Policy—We are committed to relentlessly improving how we meet customer requirements and develop our employees.

Leadership Traits

- **Energy**—positive energy in good times and especially bad times
- **Edge**—the ability to make the tough calls
- **Passion**—for being a leader, for our business, and for your area of responsibility

- **Energize**—the ability to create an environment that energizes your team
- **Execute**—the ability to deliver results
- **Resiliency**—the ability to bounce back quickly from setbacks

For more on Able Aerospace, including bonuses, exclusive content, and tools, visit **Bonus. YourMostImportantNumber.com.**

Value-Creation MINDset

Agreement on the purpose of each of these alignment tools is critically important if you want to create the most value as an organization. Once you have your senior leadership team aligned on the tenets covered in this chapter, you will need to get agreement on how you do the work of maintaining alignment, relentlessly improving, and doing the right work in the right order at the right time. We'll discover this in the forthcoming chapters.

You may be wondering what it feels like to be this intentional as a senior leadership team. Talking through these exercises requires a new level of transparency and vulnerability.

Talking through these exercises requires a new level of transparency and vulnerability.

You can no longer have a need to be the smartest person in the room. You also have to be willing to be uncomfortable at times and provide strong support in and out of meetings for each team member. Most importantly, this type of transformation requires buy-in from all senior leaders, especially the CEO.

We once worked with a client with a manufacturing business where the CEO was the only person who didn't buy into the alignment tools. Sure, he worked with the senior leadership team to create them, but in day-to-day operations, he regularly behaved in ways that were counterproductive (and sometimes downright demoralizing) to team members. This caused stress and frustration throughout the ranks.

The misaligned team modeled a culture of autonomy where everyone did what was right in his or her own eyes (see Figure 1.3).

Figure 1.3

After using the MIND Methodology for about two months, the CEO began to understand the need to reinforce and live the alignment tools in a positive, productive way, rather than blasting team members for getting things wrong. This realization at the top started a tremendous change in the culture, which was palpable to the whole team. In return, the team began to create value even faster by being more engaged and releasing positive, productive energy.

This aligned team modeled a culture of synergy where people embodied trust and collaboration (see Figure 1.4).

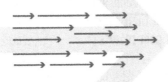

Figure 1.4

The most critical foundational element we have covered so far is for your senior leadership team to commit to making all of their work support the improvement of your organization's MIN. If you continually test this with your team and course correct when it is not happening, you are on your way. This requires a commitment from every senior leadership team member to think and act in this way.

Imagine the possibilities when every person on your senior team comes to meetings with a strong, ongoing plan backed up by actions to significantly improve your MIN. You know you are doing the work right when the MIN is improving. This is quite a departure from how most operate, which is focusing on just keeping the machine running as is.

In unhealthy environments, most of the time, senior teams point to forces outside of their control to blame for poor results.

While there can be extraordinary market forces adversely impacting your MIN, most gaps in performance are caused by the decisions a senior team is making or choosing not to make. As we've all learned, indecision is also a decision—a decision to choose to stay exactly where you are. At the end of the day, if you don't get this stuff aligned at the top of the organization, misalignment and lack of accountability will cascade throughout your organization.

In unhealthy environments, most of the time, senior teams point to forces outside of their control to blame for poor results.

A powerful way to improve the decision-making capability of any senior leadership team is to think in terms of *organizational structure* bottlenecks. This is different from *process* bottlenecks where you are eliminating waste and improving workflow. Organizational structure bottlenecks refer to the ability of the organization's functional structure to support or limit the ability to create value.

Organizational structure components can include strategy, supply chain, manufacturing, or supportive functions, such as sales, marketing, and finance. For example, if you have more customer orders than your operations can produce, then there will be one aspect of operations identified as the current bottleneck (see Figure 1.5).

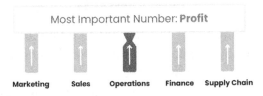

Figure 1.5

In this illustration, operations is the organizational structure bottleneck that is currently holding back improvements to the MIN more than all other functions within the organization

In order to create the most value as an organization, your senior leadership team should be laser-focused on identifying and eliminating the current organizational structure bottleneck, so they are able to resolve and move their attention to the next one. A structural bottleneck is a moving target that never goes away.

As your team gets better at having this conversation, you will be able to anticipate and predict organizational structure bottlenecks well into the future. As a result, this proactive approach will minimize the impact and grow your Most Important Number even faster. We will explore this concept further in Chapter Three.

The MIND Methodology provides a way to objectively decide where to focus and do the right work at the right time and in the right order. The following chapters provide proven ways to get a higher percentage of your team members doing this type of work.

Time for Takeaways

In companies that use the MIND Methodology as their business operating system, we do something at the end of each MIND Meeting™. We ask each person to share their "Biggest Takeaway." This means we want them to identify the most striking thing they heard in any meeting that they believe will create the most value for the organization. This concept is designed to continually improve each team member's ability to think about and create value faster for the organization. This Biggest Takeaway exercise makes the transformation a shared experience, often ranked as the best part of the meeting.

In line with this thinking, we'll end each chapter with our Biggest Takeaways. Reviewing this list will drive the truths deeper.

Biggest Takeaways from Chapter One

- Alignment at the top is critical to creating the most value in the organization.
- Alignment around the organization's Most Important Number is a core foundational element of the MIND Methodology.
- Alignment tools are popular but incredibly underutilized to drive financial results.
- Regular discussions about the current organizational structural bottleneck improve the decision-making capability of the senior leadership team.

- This journey will develop the value-creation MINDset so team members are focused on the right work in the right order at the right time.

2

How We Agree to Do the Work Matters

Unpacking Your Most Important Numbers and Drivers™

Ready for a one-question quiz? On the topic of value creation, what's the number one thing missing from most organizations?

Got your answer?

Here's mine: intentionality.

Very few organizations have leadership teams aligned around their Most Important Number. Even fewer have adopted an intentional way (or a consistent method) of doing the work of improving their MIN applicable to all teams.

Many senior leadership team members say they want to grow profits, cash flow, revenue, or impact on their clients' lives. While they work hard to create this, they still struggle to experience the value they know is possible. These organizations aren't intentional about *how their teams do the work of improving what is most important.* Not getting this right can feel like you're constantly rebuilding rooms in a house of cards.

The right management operating methodology solves this by aligning and energizing team members within your organization around improving what's most important. An ineffective management operating system often elevates process and activity more than improving what's most important. In other words, checking the boxes becomes the goal over achieving the desired result.

Pursuing goals is quite different from staying aligned. Sure, there are a plethora of goal-based and process-based business tools and systems to help companies grow, but most perpetuate the same low levels of engagement reported over the past few decades. Checking all the boxes doesn't matter if you don't get the desired result.

The Gallup Poll has regularly reported employee engagement under 30 percent for nearly the past twenty years (Gallup.com). When you remove the engaged and actively disengaged from the numbers, it leaves more than half of all workers "not engaged."

According to Gallup, not being engaged is defined as "psychologically unattached to their work and company. These employees put time, but not energy or passion, into their work."

Why is this important?

It's difficult to expect great financial (or impact) results in an organization with more than half of employees disengaged.

Often leaders are given some set of outcomes to achieve, but it's left to the leader to decide how to do the work of achieving it with their team. This can lead to a multitude of ways to achieve outcomes within a single organization—sometimes at the cost of something else in the organization. Strong leaders usually achieve solid results, and average leaders often miss their targets.

As noted in the Introduction, the right leader can make just about anything work. When you replace a strong leader who has a history of measurable results with an average leader, the metrics often start to suffer. This puts your company at risk because you resort to putting all your hope in a strong leader rather than a strong operating system.

When strong leaders leave, they often take success out the door with them. However, there's a way to protect your business. By integrating the right operating system across all team members, you spread the risk.

If and when strong leaders leave, the results of the remaining teams don't drop like a rock. Also, average leaders are quickly poised to develop into strong leaders. This builds a leadership culture where everyone is responsible and accountable.

Energizing Your Team

Ideally, we have always wanted each employee to think of themselves as the CEO of their own role. In essence, each person is growing a business within a business by continually creating more value over time. One of the biggest mistakes companies make is allowing employee development to be disconnected from the work they were hired to do.

The common approach to employee development tends to consist of enrolling in a class or program or reading the latest book on a relevant topic with the hope the team member will transfer their learnings into the workplace to improve results. I'm not referring to basic skills or technical training to perform a task. We're talking about applying skills and leadership capability to continually increase the value each individual and team creates. At any point in time, there will always be several actions individuals and teams can take to increase the value they create.

We've found the most effective development opportunities generally present themselves when you realize you don't currently have the capability to address something or to achieve a particular result. To improve the top level or one of your functional team's Most Important Numbers at the quickest pace possible, each team member has to be aware of and on the leading edge of where they should develop next based on how they can best contribute to improving their MIN.

With this approach, employee development is always connected to the results you're trying to achieve. You know you're doing the right employee development work when the results prove it. There are different types of development work, from increasing the capabilities of team members to improving how they are perceived and interact with other team members. The best development opportunities always show up *while* doing the work.

In organizations focused on improving results, employees tend to approach work by spending much of their time firefighting or simply reacting to whatever shows up. In this scenario, it's extremely hard to develop every team member intentionally and effectively. Ideally, every team member will be able to identify and work on their next one to three professional or personal development opportunities to create higher levels of value.

The most common practice we've observed is for managers to ask their team members to independently set development goals to work on over the next several months. This goal-setting process tends to *not* lead to adding capabilities team members need to create more value for the entire organization.

When a team is doing the *right* work, they'll always be able to see where they need more capability from current or additional team members, adding value to improve their MIN faster. It's most effective when individual team members' goals are agreed upon by the entire team.

Intentionally or unintentionally, every organization has its own unique way of getting things done. Most embrace some form of a goal-setting process.

For a moment, put yourself in your employees' shoes as they go through the goal-setting process. We often hear from employees that they set one to three goals each quarter, get them approved by their manager, follow up with their manager at the end of the quarter, and repeat. It always feels better for the senior leader who mandated the process than it does for most employees going through it.

In a short time, this process devolves into a check-the-box exercise. It becomes more about the completion of the task rather than the value created. We have audited thousands of goals in all types and sizes of organizations, and very few were thoughtful or connected to creating value for the organization. Unfortunately, the majority of employees expressed stress about mandated goal-setting processes and struggled to find the "right" goals.

We've spoken to many senior leaders who say their approach to goal setting is working great, but when we interview their employees, it is always a different story. Often CEOs say everyone is winning on their goals, but the company isn't going anywhere. This is a clear sign the goal-setting process isn't working.

Nearly all teams want to win because it feels great to win. Humans are hardwired to win. If employees thought traditional goal setting would really help them win, they would embrace the process. Not to mention, it requires monumental effort to sustain a goal-setting process for all team members within an organization.

In our own business, we were able to do it in the past, but few of our counterparts could. It took huge amounts of energy and time to sustain traditional goal-setting processes. The few times when we backed off from enforcing the process, most of our employees drifted away from it. We realized traditional goal setting wouldn't stand the test of time.

There are too many variables that can derail it. A highly effective, outcome-achieving process should take on a life of its own without enormous efforts by the senior team to keep it going. Your teams should be building their own momentum when it comes to getting better results, not waiting for you to keep them motivated.

Know What is Expected 100 Percent of the Time

We've already been exploring the "MIN" of MIND (Most Important Number). We've also touched on the "D" of MIND in reference to Drivers. When we combine these two foundational elements, we have what is known as the MIND Methodology (Most Important Number and Drivers). The MIND Methodology reflects how teams do the work of improving what is most important. In other words, it is agreeing on the work which will create the most value, aligning on how we make decisions, and to what we hold each team member accountable.

Practicing the MIND Methodology allows every team member to know what is expected of them and their performance in meeting those expectations 100 percent of the time.

Let's take a deeper dive into the MIND Methodology and start with how teams do the work of improving what is most important. One element of the MIND Methodology is reflected in how teams think, act, and behave in meetings. When a team meets, their MINDset needs to reflect intentionality to create as much value as possible. The MIND Methodology includes a component called the "MIND Meeting™." This is a specific meeting where each team participates in organizing their work around what is most important (see Figure 2.1).

Figure 2.1

MIND Meeting

Have you ever been to a meeting where people talk about everything they are doing ad nauseam, and it has very little to do with what you are doing or with moving the business forward?

You're not alone.

Often meetings are spent with team members justifying their work, which can be a major waste of time. When this happens, most others check out and disengage during the meeting. Morale declines, not to mention profitability.

If you calculated the cost of salaries in the room over the course of a year, you'd surely be seeking an alternative.

If you calculated the cost of salaries in the room over the course of a year, you'd surely be seeking an alternative. The MIND Meeting does the complete opposite. It increases morale, not to mention profitability. This is why it's one of the most supportive elements of the MIND Methodology.

The cadence of the MIND Meeting can be weekly, biweekly, or monthly. We generally start MIND Meetings in a weekly cadence, and as the team begins to accomplish more work in less time, we are able to move the meetings out to biweekly or monthly.

Some organizations conduct MIND Meetings with their senior leadership team only. Other companies have all functional teams participate in respective MIND Meetings. Because the time is spent laser-focused on work to support what's most important, every member has value to contribute.

Check-In

The shortest part of a MIND Meeting is what we call the "Check-In." During the Check-In (which tends to take about fifteen minutes of a one-hour meeting), each team member shares:

1. Their "Biggest Win" from the previous week.
2. Information the team needs to know to help other team members make better decisions.
3. "What I need help with" or what areas a team member is seeking assistance or information from others requiring team input.

The Check-In is an essential part of the MIND Methodology and develops each team member to think in terms of creating more value. We have found it is helpful to have each team member add their Check-In information twenty-four hours in advance of the meeting, so all members' input is available to read through prior to the meeting start.

Let's walk through the details of how it works.

Biggest Wins

The first segment of the Check-In is celebrating "Biggest Wins." This creates a culture of focusing on what is working well and building on it. These wins can be personal or professional achievements or exciting news. At first, some team members don't feel comfortable talking about their own wins, so they point out wins they noticed other team members having.

Some examples of the Biggest Wins our clients have shared include winning a big contract, a team member's daughter having a successful first day at school, finding a new vendor for a critical supply chain item, observing a colleague's personal commitment to the end result, purchasing a new house, reducing maintenance expenses by 20 percent last quarter, a new office manager far exceeding expectations, among many others.

Better Decisions

After a team member shares their Biggest Win, they share what information the team needs to know to make better decisions. This segment builds a new skill and deepens team members' understanding of what information may be useful to other team members. They put themselves in their coworkers' shoes to really think about what knowledge they have that can help others in their roles. This can also be information to help make a critical decision.

We've found most people are not naturally adept at determining what constitutes a critical decision. To simplify, we define a critical decision as "anything with the potential to materially impact the MIN." When your team members bring the information they believe others should know to make better or critical decisions, you get a clear look into their thinking. As a leader, this gives you the exact starting point from which to develop each of your team members around decision-making capability.

When building the muscle of what information to share during the Check-In to help your teammates make better decisions, it usually falls into one of two camps. When teams first begin with MIND Meetings, sharing tends to be related to just doing their job. Some examples include:

- "We got our financial reports out on time."
- "We had a good team meeting today."
- "I am working on solving a problem."
- "I am working Monday through Friday this week."

Over time, the information provided to help other team members make better decisions evolves into information to directly help other team members achieve better results. These more-evolved examples include:

- "I learned in the past two weeks our distributors need more help from our account managers."
- "We won a larger than expected contract which will have a big impact on operations and supply chain."
- "I developed a new fixture to cut assembly time by 50 percent and can be applied to twelve other product lines."

See the difference?

Learning to continually make better decisions is a never-ending journey. How much better are you today compared to a year ago regarding making decisions designed to create value? Are you better than you were five years ago or ten years ago? The point is it takes time to develop this decision-making muscle.

A big part of your job as a leader is to develop your team members to continually improve their value-creating, decision-making capability. It may have taken you a long time to develop your current level of value-creating decision-making capability. If you are intentional, the MIND Methodology has proven to significantly help speed up this development.

Need Help?

The last segment of the Check-In is "what I need help with." Generally speaking, the help needed during the Check-In should be general and not directly apply to the second part of the MIND Meeting (where we explore "improving what's most important" and move over to the MIN and Driver conversation).

Asking for help during the Check-In should apply to the majority or all of the team members. If not, you can end up having a bunch of two- or three-person meetings within your team meeting. This is not a productive use of the team's Check-In.

Examples of asking for general help can include:

- "Does the team agree to roll out a program on this date?"
- "Is the team okay with hiring three people in the accounting department?"
- "Please do the employee satisfaction survey, and send me the results by this date."

- "Please inform your team that open enroll-ment for health insurance begins on this date."
- "Adjust your timelines to move into our new facilities because the date has been changed."

This segment isn't a deep dive on the need for help. Rather, it's designed to set up the issue for the next section of the MIND Meeting that you'll encounter in the next segment.

The entire Check-In is designed to ensure every team member has a voice. The process strengthens the value of their contributions to the team.

In senior leadership team meetings, there are often meeting dominators, where two or three people collectively speak 80 percent of the time. As you get closer to frontline teams, many team members lack the confidence to speak up. The Check-In portion of the MIND Meeting is designed to move all team members toward having an equal voice at all levels within your organization.

In terms of the breakdown of time between the "Check-In" and the "What's Most Important," we rec-ommend approximately 25 percent of the scheduled meeting time spent on the Check-In and 75 percent of the time spent improving what's most important.

Here is an illustration of what the cadence looks like (see Figure 2.2 below).

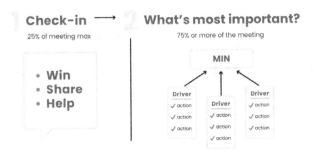

Figure 2.2

Improving What's Most Important

Once the Check-In is completed, the team transitions to improving what's most important. Every team has agreed on their Most Important Number. This is also true for developing categories of work or Drivers used to support improving each team's MIN. If you want to increase your team's motivation for doing the right work to improve what is most important, your team needs to be actively involved in *designing* the work.

Right Work, Right Order, Right Time

In most organizations, the goals and objectives are handed down with little or no input from the team charged with accomplishing them. As a result, most teams tend to have a low level of buy-in and lack a culture of accountability.

Remember the connection regarding the decades of general lack of engagement identified by the Gallup Poll results previously shared? There is a direct correlation between employees' involvement in designing their work and their attitude toward having a culture of accountability.

According to a November 2020 *Harvard Business Review* article, "91 percent of employees would say 'effectively holding others accountable' is one of their company's top leadership development needs."

Surprisingly, employees say *management* should be better at holding others accountable, yet Gallup's statistics show traditional methods are not working. Why? Most managers' perception of "holding accountable" resembles parenting, not managing and leading.

The few companies that truly put team members in a position to design and contribute to how they do their work end up with employees engaging in the work and, more powerfully, living up to their potential at work.

You might be thinking it's easier said than done. However, if each team member knows their Most Important Number, it can be easier. Here's why: When they do, they can now develop their own custom Drivers to support their MIN. Remember, Drivers are those categories of work within the team's control (or those they can significantly influence) in order to improve their MIN. Drivers for each team can vary significantly from other teams' Drivers depending on what their MIN is.

Here are some examples of different functional teams' Most Important Numbers and supporting Drivers:

Senior Leadership Team MIN: Net Profit
- Supporting Drivers
  - Strategy
  - Service delivery
  - People development
  - Culture
  - Management operating system

Finance MIN: Cash Flow
- Supporting Drivers
  - Financial reporting
  - Collections
  - Payables
  - Financing
  - Strategic relationships

Operations MIN: Gross Profit
- Supporting Drivers
  - Quality
  - Delivery
  - Safety
  - Waste/scrap elimination
  - Technology

Marketing MIN: Qualified Leads
- Supporting Drivers
  - Communicating our value

- o Paid marketing
- o Organic traffic
- o Testimonials
- o Brand awareness

HR MIN: Percent of Seats Filled with Capable People
- Supporting Drivers
  - o Employee onboarding
  - o Employee development
  - o Compensation
  - o Performance management
  - o Leadership development

The process of determining which Drivers your team can leverage to move the MIN forward can take some time. As with any methodology, the mindset around the systems and methods is critical and intentional. Once your team has developed a set of Drivers to leverage to improve your MIN, your team then answers the following questions for each Driver:

- **Question 1**: On a scale from one to ten, how well are we leveraging this Driver today to improve our MIN?
- **Question 2:** What would a "ten" state look like (meaning: there is no way to leverage it any better than we can think of today)?

Having facilitated these conversations with hundreds of teams over the past several years, it's common for teams to rate how well they are currently leveraging each Driver as "low" (somewhere between one to three out of ten). This is actually a good thing in most cases because it allows the team to make significant improvements to their MIN relatively quickly.

Once your team has rated each of the Drivers, you select which ones to label "In Focus." It's impossible to significantly improve everything at once, so your team should focus on *no more than three* "In Focus" Drivers at any point in time.

During the "improve what's most important" part of the meeting, your team gives attention to the In Focus Drivers by creating "Action Items" to continually improve how well the team is leveraging each driver to improve their MIN. There is no end to how well a team can leverage Drivers to improve their MIN. It's the team's job to continually discover these improvements. Action Items are where the rubber really meets the road. This is where we execute on our agreement regarding the work we *can* do and narrow it to the work we *should* do. We'll further explore Action Items in the next chapter.

In comparing the MIND Methodology to traditional goal setting, the MIND Methodology focuses on the completion of goals and actions to improve the Most Important Number, rather than checking the box saying we fulfilled what we said we would, regardless of whether the work made a measurable difference. While widely practiced in many organizations, we recognize traditional goal setting is not often thought through in most cases. In contrast, the

MIND Methodology engages your team to go after that one number that, above all others, determines whether you are winning or losing the game.

This process also provides a vehicle for the team to identify viable Drivers they can leverage to improve their MIN. Over time, as the thinking of your team evolves, you may reforecast your MIN, commit to it, and continually improve how well each member leverages each Driver to achieve your MIN.

This approach to doing the work of improving what is most important is simple, energizing, and helps your teams do what they already want to do (which is win). It also influences your team to feel successful because they accomplished challenging work and increased motivation with each member involved in every step of developing the work.

MIN Forecast

The MIN Forecast refers to where you want your MIN to be over time. If your MIN is cash flow, and you want to increase it by 30 percent over the next twelve months, this is your MIN Forecast. As your teams get better at doing the work of improving what is most important, it's common to reforecast MIN projections.

The three questions to keep in mind:

1. Where are we now?	This refers to the current value of your MIN.
2. Where are we going?	This refers to where you would like the value of your MIN to be in the future.
3. How will we get there?	This refers to how well your team leverages your Drivers to achieve your forecasted MIN over time.

In light of these three questions, the work of improving what is most important quickly becomes self-sustaining. You're now able to keep building momentum without a Herculean effort from the senior leadership team to keep it going. The building of forward-moving momentum shifts to your functional teams. Each team also creates a handful of vital Key Performance Indicators (KPIs) to track but retains their one true North Star, their MIN, telling them if they are winning or losing.

Your team does the work of improving their MIN through developing one another to make better decisions and improving how well they're able to leverage Drivers. Doing the work of improving what is most important is the foundation for the MIND Methodology.

For additional resources on this topic, including exclusive content and proven tools, visit **Resources. YourMostImportantNumber.com.**

MIND Software

In an attempt to stay on task in meetings, many companies use some form of technology or tool to help them organize or manage their time and progress. This can be as simple as a shared Google Doc or a more complex program or app. Regarding technology-based tools, the most critical part of doing the work is the methodology, or the operating system (methods), you use to do your work. Once you have established a methodology effectively working across your teams to achieve great results, then technology and tools matter.

Tools are necessary to more effectively sustain and scale. We've all seen initiatives come and go because of the lack of discipline required to sustain them. To be clear, the MIND Methodology is used for organizational alignment, decisions, and accountability, while the actions and change occur outside the meeting. You need both—the methodology and tools—to sustain over time.

In response to the need to sustain both, we developed software to mirror the MIND Methodology elements, which makes it significantly easier to sustain and scale. As we have explored how to think about and interact with the essential components of the MIND Methodology, including MINs, Drivers,

Action Items, and MIND Meetings, it is easy to see how complex the management and dissemination of information and progress can be. Complexity is why so many goal-driven initiatives lose steam.

Our software is designed to not only make the MIND Methodology easy to sustain and scale but also to have the ability to access and identify any and every element of the MIND Methodology within any of your teams in a matter of seconds.

This level of transparency at your fingertips keeps your team members aligned. It also helps your cross-functional teams engage and work together more effectively. The right tools are invaluable to sustain and scale an effective way of doing things as well as to reduce the administrative efforts to do so.

In the forthcoming chapters, we'll explore several other supportive organizational elements of the MIND Methodology, including strategy, intentional culture, leadership development, and performance management. Now that we've established the foundation for how teams do the work of improving what is most important, we can build the other MIND Methodology elements.

Biggest Takeaways from Chapter Two

- Be intentional about how your team members do the work of improving what is most important.
- Don't make process more important than what is most important.

- Traditional goal setting struggles to stand the test of time.
- Develop your team members to be the CEO of their own roles.
- Meetings should be energizing and 100 percent focused on accelerating value creation.
- Leverage Drivers to improve your team's Most Important Number.
- Always have good answers for where you are at, where you are going, and how you will get there.

3

Get Your Teams Pulling in the Same Direction

Every Team Is a Business within a Business Working Together to Create the Most Value

In 1998, Great Britain's crew team set a goal to win the Olympic gold medal in the upcoming 2000 Olympics. This was only a two-year time frame to transform every aspect of their training.

They developed a simple question to filter how they worked together to achieve what appeared to be an impossible goal: "Will it make the boat go faster?" By filtering every thought and action through this lens, their results began improving. Lo and behold, they won the gold medal at the Sydney Olympics in 2000, proving that clarity on what was most important to make the boat go faster was delivered!

If you were to ask each of your team members how they measure the value they create, what would they say? For sure, each of your teams should be creating more value than they are being paid, or you could quickly run into financial problems. By not being clear about the value each of your teams creates, you're missing a big opportunity to increase the value of your organization as a whole. I regularly hear senior leaders complain they know their organization can perform significantly better than they currently are, but this higher level of performance seems to remain out of reach.

Having the right Most Important Number for each of your teams is the most effective way to measure the value each team was designed to create. It's also the most effective way to keep your teams focused on continually *increasing* the value they create. One challenge I see managers face is when multiple teams appear to be doing great work, but they are not collectively going in the same direction.

This is similar to an ocean liner being pulled by ten tugboats going in different directions. The result is no movement. This is a frustrating experience for everyone involved. When it becomes the norm, achievers and producers exit the company. We're all hardwired for progress, and when we don't achieve it, we go elsewhere.

Thankfully, there is a solution.

No Sideways Energy

As the top-level (senior leadership) team's MIN cascades to the front lines, each functional team MIN should measurably improve the MIN of the next level up. This is the best way to ensure all teams are pulling in the same direction when it comes to value creation. This concept is illustrated in Figure 3.1 below.

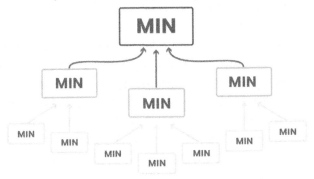

Figure 3.1

Notice how every department is pointed in the same direction. There is no sideways energy. Progress is palpable, and, therefore, team engagement is high.

Although this diagram is ideal, a high percentage of teams are not fully focused on creating the most value they can for the organization, which often leads to misalignment.

A great example of this was working with a client where the engineering department was a constant source of frustration for the senior leadership team. The senior leadership team's MIN was EBITDA (earnings before interest, taxes, depreciation, and amortization), and they wanted more new products to drive improvements in EBITDA.

The engineering team did not have a MIN and spent most of the time fighting proverbial fires in manufacturing and design, thereby developing ROI (return on investment) products. Once their MIN was determined as improvements in gross profit margins, they quickly started pulling in the same direction the company wanted to go. Out of hundreds of new product options, they only developed the ones with the highest ROI. They also focused on streamlining the manufacturing processes, saving over $1 million in the first nine months of having a MIN.

It's important for each team to do the right work in the right order at the right time to have the greatest impact on improving their MIN.

The right work is defined as the work creating the most value in both the short term and the long term. When you collect all of your team's ideas and observations in pursuit of creating more value, capture them in categories of work your team should be able to leverage (a.k.a. "Drivers"). We know teams juggle many projects and ideas to try out at any given time. The challenge is knowing what work to leverage and when.

The activities or steps you will take to best leverage a Driver are "Action Items." You can have dozens to hundreds of actions your team members can take to improve the team's MIN. The right work will be the actions creating more value than all the other actions at any point in time.

This is a continually moving target, and the MIND Methodology is designed to develop teams at all levels within your organization to get better at prioritizing the right work in the right order at the right time. All teams have limited capacity, so it is important they are engaged in the highest value-creating work at every point in time.

As discussed in Chapter Two, a team can be responsible for several Drivers. All actions designed to improve the MIN should be captured as Action Items within these Drivers. You can't effectively improve everything all at once, so it is important to have no more than three Drivers "In Focus" at any point in time. The In Focus Drivers should be the ones that, when improved, will create more value than the Drivers not currently in focus.

Just because a Driver is not in focus does not mean there is no supportive work going on. It also doesn't mean we are ignoring it. The goal for all Drivers not currently in focus is to never slip backward in how the team leverages those Drivers to improve their MIN. The current business conditions will always dictate which Drivers will be labeled In Focus for a given team.

For example, if your current business situation shows profitable revenue significantly below forecast due to qualified leads dropping off, and your team's MIN is net profit, then the Driver titled "Marketing" should be labeled "In Focus." You may also create a "Sales" Driver and label it "In Focus" because getting better at closing the leads you have will help close the gap on your current revenue shortfall. Action Items are then assigned to team members who are positioned to improve how well they are leveraging—in this case, your marketing and sales Drivers—to improve your MIN (see Figure 3.2).

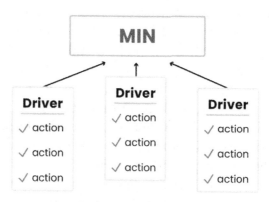

In-Focus Drivers ensure actions are taken that significantly improve the MIN

Figure 3.2

All team members' actions and behaviors are influenced by viewing their work through the lens of *how will this improve our MIN, both in the short run and long run?* Further, their mentality should be influenced by thinking, "Is the work we are focusing on today going to improve our MIN more than any other work we could be doing right now?"

Ideally, every functional team should be aligned and in perfect balance with all other teams. When referring to balance, I'm referring to each team being in perfect support of one another and focused on creating the most value as an organization at any point in time.

In reality, there is usually an imbalance. We've seen many cases where sales is bringing in more work than operations can produce or deliver. As a result, they upset more and more customers because they can't deliver the product or service when promised. Intentionally thinking about the ideal organizational structure and keeping it in balance is an opportunity missed by many small and mid-sized organizations. Large organizations are not immune either.

It is more difficult to maintain alignment the larger the organization becomes. However, when using the MIND Methodology, the complexity of managing alignment is significantly removed because we've been intentional about focusing on the right work in the right order at the right time.

Outcomes

The MIND Methodology also espouses an effective way of designing for balance and alignment by first focusing on desired outcomes. Desired outcomes are the measures for the overall organization, as well as for each department or team. This measured outcome, the MIN, shows whether a team is winning or missing the mark. Although there may be many desired outcomes or measures for a team, this primary outcome or measure reflects the value the organization or team creates.

Structure

Once MINs are determined for all departmental teams, focus shifts to the structure. This encompasses all organizational functions, departments, locations, alliances, allocation of resources, and roles with associated outcome-based responsibilities. Once outcomes and the functional structure are clearly defined, we then focus attention on the people. Most senior leadership teams tend to want to start with what their people can and cannot do, and most of the time, they get stuck on who is in the role rather than what the role should accomplish.

In a for-profit business, you may choose your MIN as growing net profit, which tends to be a fairly common outcome for a for-profit business. Your very next question should be, "What is the ideal organizational structure to achieve growing net profit, given your mix of products and services?" Once you've answered this question, focus your thinking on a different question, "What are the most important outcomes, or MINs, for each team or function within its structure?"

Next, identify the ideal roles and associated outcome-based responsibilities within each team or function. Responding to these inquiries can generally take some time as you begin to recognize how the functions and parts fit together. The last consideration is to list all strategic alliances, agreements, locations, and allocation of resources for each part of your ideal structure.

People

Once you've designed your ideal functional structure to support the desired outcomes with clearly defined roles, only then do you work hard to ensure each functional role is filled with people who have the resources and are capable of achieving the outcome-based responsibilities. Organizational design should be incredibly intentional in order to create the most value possible for your organization. Following this process will provide a clear roadmap for recruiting and developing your current and future team members.

Virtually every employee I've met has expressed wanting more clarity around their performance and what is expected. Most employees crave clarity around their team's goals and their specific, outcome-based responsibilities. This approach is foundational to the MIND Methodology and creates the conditions for employees to know what is expected of them 100 percent of the time (see Figure 3.3).

Outcomes
What are our desired outcomes?

Structure
Do we have the right structure to achieve our desired outcomes?

People
Are our resources appropriately applied within our structure?

Figure 3.3

Knowing the Lay of the Land

Connecting MINs throughout an organization is an incredible way to ensure all teams are pulling in the same direction and lays the foundation for accelerating the value your organization creates over time. Once your MIN structure is in place, along with utilizing MIND Meetings, you can more easily solve several common problems, such as busting silos, creating effective cross-functional collaboration, quickly and effectively seeing the lay of the land, identifying what each team is doing to improve their MIN, and so much more.

As discussed in Chapter Two, the MIND Methodology makes everything team members want to do much easier. It also allows an organization as a whole (or specific functional teams) to learn to pivot quickly and effectively to respond to changes in the internal or external environments.

In most organizations, leaders have a good idea of what their teams need to do, and they lead the team to do it their way.

Maybe you've seen this before?

If there are ten leaders, there are likely ten different ways of doing the work within their respective teams. These differences can be subtle to dramatic. The more leaders we have, the more opportunities to differ in how work is accomplished. By addressing work by different methods, imagine how long it takes an employee transferring from one team to another to get up to speed regarding how their new team does their work.

It can take weeks or months to settle in (and generally much frustration because *how we do the work* is not generally transparent under normal, prevailing conditions). When the MIND Methodology is common across all teams, there is virtually no time required to get up to speed on how any team does the work of improving what is most important as you move throughout the organization. The goal is to make the time for a new team member to get up to speed go from months to minutes.

A common "side effect" of the MIND Methodology is that cross-functional collaboration starts to happen organically between functional teams. With your employees speaking the same language around how they do the work and each team having a clear MIN to measure the value they are creating, it's natural to reach out to other teams to help improve each other's MIN even faster.

When a team is looking for every opportunity to improve their MIN, they quickly see interdependencies with other teams. Information becomes more fluid upstream and downstream. Most of the time, teams start doing this on their own because it is natural for teams to be curious about what other teams are doing to improve their MIN. Using the MIND Methodology feels really natural for teams, and as a result, it takes on a life of its own.

How do you know the MIND Methodology is working?

1. As you look to assess how well your teams are performing, what information do you want to know?
2. Are you getting a return on your investment in the team (achieving their MIN)?
3. What are they doing to improve their MIN?
4. What information are they sharing to make better decisions?
5. Where are they winning or losing?

6. Are they assigning actions and executing their plan to improve the MIN?
7. What other information do you want to know to see if things are on track or not?
8. Do you feel confident you could answer these questions for all of your teams?
9. If so, how long does it take you to currently get this information to all of your teams?

This is a simple and effective way of doing the work to continually create more value over time. We recognize tools are still required to make it easy to sustain and scale. Having one place to engage and collect all the information resulting from the MIND Methodology makes it easy to see a complete lay of the land in your organization in just minutes, as well as get up to speed with what any team is doing to create more value.

Once all teams are connected through their Most Important Numbers, it becomes very easy to see what they are capable of doing. This makes creating and executing a strategy significantly more effective for two reasons. First, you will have a clear view of what your teams can and cannot do today. This leads to more effective strategic decisions built from where you are currently, not where you think you should be. Second, you will have an effective way to connect strategy to execution and make it a living, breathing process.

More Bottlenecks, More Case Studies

In Chapter One, we introduced the concept of *organizational structure bottlenecks*, which are different from process bottlenecks. As you may recall, process bottlenecks are designed to improve workflow, which can improve quality, cost, delivery, safety, and customer experience. Continuous improvement philosophies and practices, like the Toyota Production System, are fantastic for value-stream mapping and addressing process bottlenecks.

When addressing organizational structure bottlenecks, the goal is to accelerate total organizational value creation. As a leader, your goal is to make this an intentional conversation generating quick and thoughtful action based on desired overall outcomes. The intent is not to focus blame or finger-point at people but at the structure supporting organization-wide value creation.

In many organizations, bottlenecks are not adequately

> The intent is not to focus blame or finger-point at people but at the structure supporting organization-wide value creation.

addressed because there is concern over how this discussion will be perceived by the people responsible for the currently blocked outcome. Rather than address it from a structural level, it tends to become a blame game as to how it became blocked or who is responsible. It can be hard to tell Mary her marketing department isn't generating enough qualified leads when she is the most senior member of the leadership team.

Usually, when the conversation occurs, it tends to add more unproductive pressure on Mary's marketing function with little to no collaboration on how the team can work to solve the problem. When the senior team approaches this challenge from an organizational structural bottleneck perspective, with the understanding that one of their primary jobs is proactively addressing these bottlenecks collaboratively, solving the problem becomes much more collaborative, productive, and far less personal.

Over the years, I have come to recognize there tend to be leaders who are "untouchable" when it comes to discussing poor results. For example, whatever outcome this leader produces is what we have to accept, and there is a culture of it not being okay to challenge them. This can happen for a variety of reasons, such as seniority, a personal relationship with the founder, partner status, their dominating or aggressive personality, their need to be the smartest person in the room, or their history of shutting ideas down that are not theirs.

This acceptance of poor results because of any reason is toxic to the organization's culture and throttles productive energy among the team. Unfortunately, this tends to cascade to the functional teams. Your senior leadership team will create value much faster by proactively seeking organizational structural bottlenecks objectively and collaboratively as part of your decision-making process.

When we started working with a for-profit, membership-based organization, it quickly became clear their current and biggest organizational bottleneck was marketing. I found it fascinating to see no one was challenging the lack of results, even though they were significantly missing their membership and revenue KPIs.

The sales team would occasionally say they needed more qualified leads, and the quick response from marketing was sales should be closing more of the leads they were given, even though the qualified lead flow was less than half of what was agreed to in the marketing MIN.

The marketing leader spent time showing activity dashboards with numbers associated with website visits, emails sent out, impressions, and free merchandise sent out, as though the swirl of "activity" was the end goal for marketing. Every time there was an attempt to discuss improving the number of qualified leads, the marketing leader immediately shut the discussion down.

Once we started discussing organizational structure bottlenecks, they began having productive, collaborative conversations around addressing the qualified lead generation challenge. For this member-based organization, we identified three main organizational structural functions:

1. Marketing
2. Sales
3. Member experience

It only took a few weeks to be able to improve each of them in a more productive and collaborative way.

In another example, a manufacturing company had not been able to get out from under their late back orders for the previous decade. Everyone stayed in their lanes and hoped for the best. Several of the senior leaders were wearing multiple hats with little to no clarity around outcome-based responsibilities. In using the MIND Methodology to determine what, more than anything else, was hindering improving the MIN, it quickly became obvious the organization's structural bottleneck was supply chain.

Raw materials used to manufacture parts were regularly delayed, and there were many unplanned, surprise shortages of supplies needed to produce and ship the final products. When challenged on the supply chain functional bottleneck, the CEO would shut the conversation down. As a result, other senior leaders became conditioned to address it by picking up the supply chain responsibilities when and where they could to keep production moving. With the best of intentions, the bottleneck was not getting resolved.

Once we started having organizational structure bottleneck discussions, we discovered the supply chain manager was involved in too many other areas. As a result, he wasn't able to fully meet the outcomes required for any of the roles. Once the supply chain manager was able to focus solely on the supply chain, the results improved almost immediately. This particular leader commented that, for the first time, he knew exactly what he was supposed to do and how good it felt to be able to spend his time focused and aligned with creating value for the organization.

Supporting the removal of organizational structure bottlenecks should be openly and objectively communicated to any and all parts of your organization. By aligning all of your organization's MINs, you'll have everyone pulling in the same direction. And by enlisting all of your leaders to identify and work to remove organizational structure bottlenecks, you'll improve your top-level Most Important Number even faster.

When your leaders collaborate cross-functionally to help each other improve their MINs and to eliminate the current structure bottleneck, they develop much faster in their ability to holistically create value for your organization.

Biggest Takeaways from Chapter Three

- Develop a value-creation MINDset in every team member.
- Every team should have a Most Important Number.
- All team MINs, by design, should support improving the organization's MIN and ensure every team is pulling in the same direction.
- The MIND Methodology encourages doing the right work in the right order at the right time.
- Drivers focus on the work your team can do to improve what is most important.

- Put the right structure in place to achieve the organization's MIN, knowing it will be a moving target.
- Develop two to four outcome-based responsibilities for each role (see Chapter 4, p. 124).
- Ensure the people in each role have the ability to achieve the required outcomes. The most effective order is outcomes, structure, then people.
- Continually address organizational bottlenecks. There will always be one function holding the organization back more than all the others.

4

Congratulations—You're 3 Percent of the Way There

Connect Your Strategy to Execution

Many senior leadership teams perform some version of an annual strategy-setting process but are less successful in connecting the dots to fully executing it. This is because it's intellectually stimulating to talk *about* strategy, but it takes more effort to clarify how to execute it as part of the process. Very few organizations regularly or effectively refer to their strategy work after the session is completed. This is a common problem in over 95 percent of the organizations we have worked with.

Questions to Consider

- How well is your team connecting strategy to execution?
- Is it yielding the results you know are possible?
- Is your leadership team living and appropriately adjusting the strategy throughout each year?
- Do each of your leaders know what they need to do (per the agreed-upon strategy) and how it supports the total value your organization creates?

These are important questions to think through in order to fully connect your strategy to execution.

The purpose of creating a living, breathing strategy is to confidently make decisions to cause sustained improvements in your organization's Most Important Number. When done effectively, these sustained improvements can be significant. Good strategy means always knowing your current status, where you are going, and how you will get there.

When working with an organization whose team has just completed their strategy session, say, "Congratulations! You are 3 percent of the way there." This is because 97 percent of the work is executing on the strategy and iterating in real time to adjust for constantly moving market conditions.

I believe strategy needs to be based on what the company can do, not solely on what the senior leadership team would like to see happen. There often tends to be a disconnect from what their organization currently has the capability to do. When this happens, there are often too many ideas and initiatives to execute properly on any of them.

In many cases, people are being asked to do things they have never done before and don't have the capability to do. It can be easy to say that something didn't work, but had the task been given to someone with the right capabilities, it would have worked.

In using the MIND Methodology, it's important for the leadership team to get fully in the groove of doing the work of improving what is most important before going through a strategy session. Having this way of *value-creation thinking* embedded into the system gives the leadership team a better idea of the organization's true capabilities. Knowing this allows the teams to execute on desired outcomes. Senior leadership teams we work with generally have a good sense for this work within eight weeks of their regularly scheduled MIND Meetings.

When the senior leadership team is ready to address strategy, it's important to have a clear purpose, framework, and rules of engagement. As previously stated, the purpose of having a strategy session is to make decisions causing sustained improvement in your organization's MIN over time. Coming to an agreement on a strategy session's purpose, framework, and rules of engagement are all critical decisions. How does your leadership team define the purpose of a strategy session?

The Five Critical Decision Categories

In using the MIND Methodology, we recognize there are decisions to be made, and then there are critical decisions. As previously noted, we define a critical decision as anything *materially impacting the MIN*. For every 100 decisions made, only about one to three of them will actually be critical. Critical decisions with the biggest impact on the MIN generally fall into five categories:

1. **Value**—Improving the perceived and actual value of your products and services.
2. **Elements**—Improving the foundational elements required to sell and deliver your products and services, including organizational structure and people.
3. **Context**—Determining where to compete and where not to compete.
4. **Pricing**—Determining pricing policies and structures.
5. **Alliances**—Identifying strategic alliances.

Decision Category One: Value

The first category, *improving the perceived and actual value of your products and services*, should be a never-ending, evergreen process. It's not uncommon for an organization to believe their customers love their products and services much more than they actually do.

As a result, many senior leadership teams make decisions to scale before they have something with enough perceived value in the marketplace to scale in the way they think it will or want it to.

Customer experience is everything, yet many leadership teams tell me they're too busy focusing on scaling than spending time on customer experience. We all know customer experience is of the utmost importance if we want to sell more of what we have to offer. If we know this to be true, why don't more organizations have resources dedicated to studying and improving customer experience? And, by the way, we're talking about both internal and external customers.

A key decision is to ensure enough resources are appropriately allocated to studying and improving your customers' experience. We see this playing out a lot in SaaS (Software as a Service) early-stage companies. In one example, we had a client who developed an application to roll out an employee development program within companies. They already decided the marketplace would respond well with little to no customer testing. They raised millions of dollars and spent it setting up marketing, sales, and operations management.

The result was the application didn't take off. When they started applying the MIND Methodology to their work, however, the majority of their efforts went into getting the product right. When they shifted to this focus, to how customers were using (or not using) the app and how to build on what was working, the monthly active users grew significantly.

Decision Category Two: Elements

Our second category, *improving the foundational elements required to sell and deliver your products and services*, involves making some critical decisions. One critical decision should include consideration of improving how each element, function, department, or team performs to balance the allocation of resources across the organization. A simple example: If you recognize you consistently have more capacity to produce products and services than you have in sales, you could decide to increase the allocation of resources to revenue-generating activities.

This could mean generating more qualified leads or increasing sales resources to close them. You may decide to study the approach to generating qualified leads and closing them to ensure you don't pour more money into something not working. In many cases, it's easy to quickly and inexpensively package and test and see what works to generate qualified leads before going all-in and potentially being wrong.

In Figure 4.1 below, the organization is heavily invested in producing its products and services and much less invested in revenue generation. In this simple example, the allocation of resources needs to be rebalanced. This may seem obvious, but you would be surprised at how few organizations have meaningful allocation of resources discussions. I am not talking about fighting over budgets to get as much as you can for your department. I'm talking about balancing resource allocation to create the most value as an organization at any point in time.

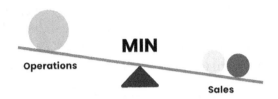

Figure 4.1

Critical decisions about team members' performance can significantly increase or decrease the value your organization creates. Leaving leaders in place for too long who don't have the capability to deliver on their role's outcome-based responsibilities are often the costliest decisions a senior leadership team can make. We know by now that choosing not to make a decision here is making a decision.

Assessing your organization's functional structure, roles within the structure, and your team members' ability to deliver on the required outcome-based responsibilities within each role has to be part of your ongoing strategy practice. Leaving a team member in place who isn't delivering on their role's responsibilities for too long is also the least caring thing you can do. It sets up the employee for inevitable failure instead

Leaving a team member in place who isn't delivering on their role's responsibilities for too long is also the least caring thing you can do.

of giving them an opportunity to be successful elsewhere, and it is demoralizing to other team members who are performing well.

I learned this lesson the hard way by leaving leaders in positions for too long where they didn't deliver, and it cost my businesses millions of dollars.

Every team member should know what is expected to be successful and how well they are performing in their respective role 100 percent of the time.

Decision Category Three: Context

Determining where to compete and not to compete is the third type of critical decision.

Even though my success in the aviation after-market business was described as wildly successful by many, it could have been so much more had my team discussed and made the right decisions in the early years. As you may recall from the Introduction, our company repaired, overhauled, and manufactured air-craft parts for commercial helicopter and fixed-wing aircraft operators worldwide. Our mission was to safely reduce aircraft operating costs, and we achieved our mission every day.

The problem was, early on, we said yes to virtually every repair request made. As a result, we developed 10,000-plus repairs over the years. Less than 100 of them made up 80 percent of our revenue at the time I sold the business in 2016. Early on, I was unaware of the opportunity to focus on only core products with big growth and profit margin opportunities.

By not being thoughtful and intentional about where to compete and not compete, we would develop a new repair, get one-quarter of 1 percent market share penetration, and then move on to the next new repair. Confession time. I love the challenge of taming the complexity of things, and we really had a complex business, so it was a ton of fun for me. Had we made better decisions in this category early on, our home run success story would have been three times larger.

Decision Category Four: Pricing

Our fourth critical decision is how the organization *makes decisions around pricing.*

What would happen if you raised your prices or lowered them? How do you know your pricing is creating the most profit for your company?

The more products and services you offer, the more challenging it is to get the pricing right across the board. To compete in different markets, you will often price the same products and services differently.

I see many companies still doing "bottom-up" pricing, meaning they pick a target profit margin, determine their costs, then set the price to hit the target profit margin. The flaw in this thinking is customers don't care what margin you want to make. They are buying *perceived value*, and, based on their perceived value, they have a limit to what they will pay for it. In other words, costs have nothing to do with what customers are willing to pay.

With all things being equal, if the customer can buy your product or service elsewhere for 5 percent less, they usually will. When it comes to pricing, it is imperative to have a pricing policy that makes sense. The most effective pricing policy for most organizations is *to charge the highest possible price while being the best value alternative and encouraging future business.*

If the market will bear $1,000 for your product or service (and not a dollar more), it doesn't matter if your cost to produce the product or service is $1,200. The customer won't pay more than $1,000. In this case, your job is to see if you can get your costs down significantly below $1,000.

The most effective pricing policy for most organizations is *to charge the highest possible price while being the best value alternative and encouraging future business.*

On the other end of the spectrum, if your costs are $200 to produce the product or service, and your bottom-up pricing approach expects a 50 percent gross profit margin, you will charge $400 and give away $600 per product or service unit you did not need to. The pricing policy outlined above will result in the highest potential impact on your MIN.

Decision Category Five: Alliances

Our fifth and final critical decision relates to identifying *strategic alliances.* Strategic alliances can vary widely depending on the size of your organization and the markets you serve. They can include access to distribution channels, distribution agreements, partnerships, certifications to perform services, trade associations, intellectual property rights, affiliate marketing channels, and more. Strategic alliances should be entered into with the intent to improve your MIN and not limit you from improving it.

Early on in my aerospace journey, there were a few larger original equipment manufacturers (OEMs) wanting us to sign agreements guaranteeing they would send us a certain amount of business. On the surface, it looked good because this was business we didn't currently have. These agreements, however, would also limit us to only doing what the OEMs would approve. Fortunately, we only entered into one of these agreements, and I wish we hadn't.

It was an effective way of limiting their competition—us! Every aircraft part we repaired directly for an aircraft operator was a part the OEM couldn't sell as a new part or repair themselves. This was not a win-win for both parties. Strategic alliances should always be win-win and designed to improve your organization's MIN.

This framework, including the top five critical decision categories for creating strategy, should ensure your senior leadership team is considering the most impactful elements linked to your organization's needs. It should fit the value your organization is trying to create to improve your MIN, not emulating someone else's best practice for creating strategy applied cookie cutter to your organization.

Getting the Most from Your Strategy Session

Before any strategy session, it's important for the senior leadership team to do their homework in order to be productively prepared. Michael Porter, author of several books and leading authority on competitive strategy, is correct in saying we are all competing for profits within the markets we serve. In other words, if you add up the total profit generated from the products and services in the markets where you compete, your job is to continually get a higher percentage of those profits.

Based on this concept, what information does your team need to know in order to make better decisions to lead to a greater share of these profits? What impacts your company's ability to compete for profits?

Some examples of information your team needs to know might include data about your customers, suppliers, competition, the regulatory environment, any and all alternatives to your product or services, potential new entrants to your market, or the risk of doing nothing.

While all of the examples above may have some impact on your ability to compete for profits, usually, only two or three will have the *most* impact on your MIN. What is the most effective set of information to look at for your organization?

We work with companies to create the foundation for effective strategic planning sessions with outcomes, not simply to create a document to shelve until the next year's session. Our strategic planning work becomes the marching orders to begin executing right away—hence the name of our company, *Execute to Win.*

The Clarity Question

When performing a strategy session for an organization, we recommend surveying the leadership team one week prior to the meeting to utilize everyone's responses as the foundation for several critical discussions during the strategic planning session.

These survey responses should be summarized and distributed to all senior leaders to review prior to the strategic planning session. This allows each leader to prepare for a much deeper discussion around the questions. Once the survey responses are explored more deeply during the strategy session, the first question for your leadership team to answer is, "What does aspirationally winning look like?"

Aspirationally winning refers to describing what is possible if everything works out perfectly for the organization given its capabilities. It can also be helpful to find out what aspirationally winning looks like for each senior leader on the team. This thought-evoking question rarely yields initial agreement. But don't despair. It's all part of the process. Alignment takes effort.

A business aspirationally winning may have several elements distinguishing it from its competitors, including impact on the communities served, healthy and functional culture, meaningful acquisitions, the organization's valuation, or a high volume of high customer satisfaction scores, among others. There is a direct link between aspirationally winning and an organization's MIN.

We've found the MIN is the easiest thing to get your team's head around when it comes to describing what aspirationally winning looks like over time. If your organization's MIN is *net profit* or *EBITDA*, then aspirationally winning could be growth in either one by 25 to 30 percent year-over-year. The more profit an organization generates, the more resources it has to make a difference in the world. The MIND Methodology ensures resources and impact are inextricably linked.

Once your team has agreed to what aspirationally winning looks like and has done their homework on the forces impacting your ability to compete for profits, your organization will be poised to make decisions driving improvements to your Most Important Number. The design of the strategy session should be based on what each individual organization needs to create the most value possible.

There's no single approach for every organization. Rather, use the questions below to create a conversation.

- What is the purpose for creating your strategy?
- What positive outcomes would you like your strategy to create for your organization?
- What are the forces most impacting your ability to compete for profits?

- What is your agreed-upon definition of aspirationally winning over the next twelve months and two to three years out?
- Where are you going to compete and not compete? This includes markets, products, and services.
- How are you going to win? What does your team have to get done this year to aspirationally win this year and set you up to win bigger in the future?
- Do you have the right functional structure to achieve your organization's desired outcomes (MINs)?
- Do you have the right people in each critical role who can deliver on their role's outcome-based responsibilities?
- What management systems do you need to win?
- How will you fully execute on your strategy?

Now for the hard part. During the strategy session, you need to have the discipline to capture all of the critical decisions made (and needed to be made) to ensure they are acted upon. It's not uncommon for a leadership team to discuss decisions needing to be made, only to never make them.

Remember how not making a decision is also a decision? There's a similar but different habit in some organizations, making decisions but never implementing them. Executing on strategy can be challenging. It takes discipline, intentionality, and regularly scheduled follow-up to ensure all decisions are executed within the appropriate area of your organization's structure.

Executing on strategy can be exponentially more complex when there isn't a common way of doing the work of improving what is most important. This is why so many organizations fail at execution. Identifying a common way for each team to organize all of the elements required to execute on their part of the strategy is a foundational key. These elements per the MIND Methodology include the following components:

- The MIN
- The set of Drivers being leveraged to improve the MIN (we denote the "In Focus" Drivers as those with the most profound impact on the MIN at this juncture)
- The set of Action Items associated with each Driver
- The set of leading indicators (KPIs) designed to facilitate effective decision-making
- The appropriate strategy elements front and center
- Input/notes from every current and past meeting... *in one place that is easily accessible*

When an effective strategy session is completed, you should be able to easily cascade the critical elements and decisions to all of the appropriate teams within the organization in a methodical and organized way. You should also be able to verify all of these elements for any team within seconds, including the work they are doing to improve their MIN.

Integrating the MIND Methodology elements for all teams within an organization simplifies the complex challenges of executing on strategy. As previously mentioned, we've developed MIND Methodology software to accomplish this. The businesses we work with love these tools at their fingertips any time they need them. Remember, your goal is to fully connect the strategy to execution and make it a dynamic, continuous practice—as natural as breathing!

For additional resources on this topic, including exclusive content and proven tools, visit **Resources. YourMostImportantNumber.com.**

Biggest Takeaways from Chapter Four

- Make how you will execute on your strategy part of your strategy-setting process.
- Ensure each leader in your organization knows how they are going to execute on their part of the strategy.
- Even if you do an annual (or more frequent) strategy deep dive, make sure it is a living, breathing process to facilitate high-value-creating adjustments in real time.
- Always know where you are, where you are going, and how you will get there.
- Have a clear purpose and rules of engagement for your strategy sessions.

- Always be improving the perceived and actual value of your products and services.
- Critical decisions (made or not made) have the potential to create the most value for your business or do the most damage.
- Set and follow a clear pricing policy.
- The right strategic alliances can be a game changer for you.

5

Is Expensive Wallpaper Good Enough for You?

Connect Culture to Financial Results

All businesses have a culture—either by intention or by accident.

Most organizational cultures appear organically simply because of the people who show up. Each new hire shapes and solidifies the culture unintentionally.

Some organizations have done the work to make their culture intentional but generally fail to tie their health and strength to the organization's financial results (and their MIN). Some are strong but not healthy or effective. They fail to encourage desired behaviors and discourage behaviors that throttle productive energy.

When a business has done its due diligence in creating a purposeful strategy executed by the full team, the next opportunity is to address the connection between organizational culture and financial results. That's the purpose of this chapter, plain and simple.

In using the MIND Methodology, we define culture as the *beliefs, accountability, practices, and decisions from which an organization creates value.* These are generally reflected in your mission, vision, purpose, and values.

Culture Questions to Consider

- How strong is your organization's culture at creating value?
- What would having a strong culture mean to you?
- Is your culture more organic or intentional?
- Can you connect the strength and application of your culture to improving financial results?
- If you asked leaders within your organization what your mission, values, and other alignment tools are, would they be able to tell you without reading them?
- More importantly, would they have solid examples of how they personally apply your organization's alignment tools to create more value for themselves, the organization, and your customers?

Alignment Tools Drive Desired Behaviors

The biggest culture challenge we see with clients (and for most organizations) is how to connect their culture to financial results.

When there are gaps in overall financial performance, it's generally caused by cultural issues within one team or function within an organization. Cultural causes of financial gaps can be found in sales, operations, customer service, finance, human resources, and other departments.

It's not uncommon for the senior leadership team to have cultural challenges (or malalignment) causing the largest financial performance gaps. When senior leadership teams are causing the largest gaps in financial performance, it is typically related to their culture of decision-making.

In Chapter One, we explored the overarching alignment tools designed to create a common culture across your organization. These alignment tools (mission, vision, purpose, and values) should act as a foundational decision filter for what your team has agreed to do, how they get things done, and where your organization is going. All of these alignment tools should be used in a way to improve your organization's top-level Most Important Number as well as any and all team MINs.

The best test for your alignment tools will be revealed when things do not go as planned. In each case, you should be able to point to one or more of your alignment tools not being properly "lived" as a clear root cause for the problem.

One of our clients with 1,400 employees across twenty-three restaurants was struggling with accountability and employee experience. The senior leadership team believed these were the two biggest opportunities to improve financial results.

When we took a deeper look, we realized not one of their alignment tools at the time addressed employee experience or accountability. Needless to say, we revised their alignment tools following our Methodology to address these opportunities.

Your alignment tools drive desired behaviors and become a fantastic management tool to hold team members accountable to sustain an intentional, strong culture.

Let's say one of your alignment tool values is *embodying a personal commitment to the end result*. A simple application of this would be a team member finishing their part of the process to get the product to your customer on time. The team member knows the date the customer needs it delivered, and there are two other processes required before it can ship.

Your team member also notices there is no one to do the next process until after the required ship date, so they rally the troops and make it happen. The customer gets what they need on time. This is a great application of *embodying a personal commitment to the end result*.

Conversely, if the team member noticed there was no one available to do the next process—knowing your product would likely ship late—and did nothing about it, this would be an opportunity for their manager to have a developmental conversation about the application of your culture. When all team members are living the cultural alignment tools, your organization will stay on mission, and team members will consistently show up in a productive way.

With many of our clients, we have found subcultures—the cultures within each team—can be significantly different from team to team. Each team's culture generally reflects the leader's style. When leadership styles vary in an organization, we tend to see that style also reflected in subcultures. Subcultures are not bad—however, they can sometimes undermine value creation or be at odds with the overarching alignment tools. When this happens, it is best to diagnose the culture more surgically.

If your organization has significant gaps in financial performance, you must first do the work of determining which function or team is contributing most to causing this condition to happen. When using the MIND Methodology, it is easy to see which functions or teams are achieving or missing their forecasted Most Important Numbers.

Without the MIND Methodology installed across all teams, you can still get there by studying financial reports and key measures for each functional team. Once you determine the functional team within the organization that is contributing most to the financial performance gap, you can diagnose and resolve it.

Numbers Never Lie

A couple of years ago, we engaged with a $100 million construction-related business based in California to determine where culture was causing the largest gap in their financial performance. They design and construct outdoor living spaces and operate in several states with approximately 450 full-time employees. Marketing, sales, project management, and design were done in-house, and construction crews were subcontracted. For two consecutive years, the company was more than 50 percent below profit projections and trending to be even worse in the coming year.

After a two-hour conversation with the CEO (as well as looking at financial and other performance data), we determined the culture within the sales function was causing the biggest gap in financial performance. While there was no measurable drop in qualified leads coming from marketing, the sales closing ratio had dropped nearly 10 percent over three years, from 28 to 19 percent. While it was obvious the closing percentage rate dropped, the cultural reasons for this drop were not so obvious.

Usually, when sales are down, there is a push for things like training, replacing or adding salespeople, refining sales tools, and increasing the number of qualified leads. Most don't approach solving the problem by finding the cultural challenge causing it.

The first step was to survey every employee within the sales organization to understand their position on beliefs, accountability, practices, and decisions impacting their ability to deliver results. The survey took ten to fifteen minutes for each leader and even less time for non-supervisory team members. The primary cause of the gap in financial performance pointed to their culture of accountability.

The survey revealed team members regularly did not do what they said they would do. There was little to no accountability for achieving a goal. Underperforming, legacy employees were considered untouchable. Last, there was no standard practice for *how* teams were held accountable.

Once we evaluated their survey responses, we transitioned our efforts to interviews and observations. We interviewed five high-performing leaders and five underperforming leaders based on their survey responses. The high-performing leaders had a developmental and supportive approach to growing each team member to achieve better results.

These leaders had a more positive outlook on how to beat the competition and grow market share. The low-performing leaders motivated their team members almost exclusively through dangling bonuses. They were not nearly as supportive and developmental as the high-performing leaders. In addition, they used excuses, such as pricing, as justification for missing the numbers.

Interestingly, we found the perception around how pricing impacts deal-closing percentage varied widely between high-performing and low-performing leaders. The high-performing leaders felt the pricing was on par with the competition to roughly 15 percent higher. They stated where pricing was higher, it was justified because of their superior product and service. Further, they reported where pricing was higher than the competition, they would likely have the lowest total costs after project overruns and fewer quality issues associated with many of the competitors. In contrast, the low-performing leaders believed pricing was 15 to 100 percent higher than the competition, and they reported this was a large contributor to their losing deals.

Once the interviews with individual leaders were completed, we attended their team meetings to observe the culture within each team. All of the high-performing leaders were happy to let us observe their meetings. In contrast, two of the low-performing leaders didn't allow us to observe their team meetings. Although there are many components to observe, such as overall energy, organization, and healthy and unhealthy behaviors, we primarily focused on accountability.

Through our observations, we found that how each team did the work of improving their sales numbers varied widely, including how accountability was enforced to achieve the numbers. Although we discovered an opportunity in creating practices to set and communicate pricing (which we addressed), our observations further confirmed the biggest opportunity was addressing their culture of accountability.

After completing the culture diagnostic work, we delivered our report with recommendations to the senior leadership team. There were several key factors we recognized in support of strengthening their culture of accountability, including the following:

- Accountability varies across the organization, with favoritism toward legacy employees.
- The organization tolerates a culture of low performance.
- Managers vary widely in their processes and practices, resulting in inconsistent results.
- There is inconsistency in what managers focus on to drive results.
- There is no standard process for enforcing accountability.
- Goal setting and coaching are not yet institutionalized at all levels.
- Excuses are prevalent with managers who could not clearly articulate how they drive accountability.

Based on our findings, we recommended the following solutions:

1. Standardize the senior leadership team meetings.
2. Standardize the regional vice president, regional sales manager, and sales manager meetings.
3. Instill key leader development with a focus on doing the work of improving what is most important.
4. Assign a personal MIN and Drivers to every salesperson.

We worked with the senior leadership team to install MIND Meetings and do the work of improving what is most important for all leaders in the organization. Accountability and alignment had to start at the top before quickly cascading it to frontline teams. Within a few months, every team and salesperson had a MIN, a set of Drivers, and participated in regularly held MIND Meetings. They now had a standard way of doing the work of improving their MIN.

As a result, we identified $9 million in increased profit potential from improving their culture of accountability. They went on to achieve $9 million in additional net profit the following year and, in total, more than three times the net profit of any preceding year.

Core Beliefs

Core beliefs are perhaps the most powerful foundational elements in connecting culture to financial results. If you don't believe something is possible to achieve within your organization, it will likely never happen.

I have decades of experience in CEO peer advisory groups observing hundreds of CEOs and what each believes is and isn't possible for their organization. It is no surprise that the CEOs presenting annual plans with 2 to 8 percent growth numbers regularly hit those numbers and just as regularly fall short. Conversely, the CEOs presenting annual plans with 20 to 50 percent-plus growth more often than not hit or beat their growth plan numbers.

With very few exceptions, I believe CEOs planning for and achieving single-digit growth can achieve so much more if they just change their core beliefs. The higher-growth CEOs seem to believe there is always a better way than they can see today, and it is their job to find it. More often than not, low-growth business leaders do not believe in the value of continuous personal and professional development. As a result, this limits their ability to accelerate the value (profit and cash flow) their organizations create.

As of the writing of this chapter, we are working with two organizations where the CEOs have a common limiting core belief. One owns a real estate brokerage business and the other an insurance and employee benefits business. When we began these engagements, both believed they were in commodity businesses, and there was little they could do to differentiate themselves from the competition. As a result, both CEOs believed that it would be difficult to profitably grow.

We are quickly changing their core beliefs to how bundled services and incredible customer service are huge differentiators. This differentiated value created for their customers allows for very profitable growth in a win-win way (for their clients and the businesses).

If you want to get an idea of what your leaders believe is possible for your business, ask them these questions:

- What does winning look like over the next twelve months for your business?

- What does winning look like two to three years out for your business?

These questions will give you a real sense of what your leadership team thinks about the potential of your business. From there, you can choose to intentionally start changing the core beliefs within your organization.

Evaluate Your Practices

What are the common practices in your organization? Which practices create the most value? Which practices create the least? Holding annual or quarterly strategy sessions is a practice. Having regular meetings of all types and at all levels in your organization is a practice—so is conducting performance reviews, celebrating wins, hiring, and goal setting.

Some practices may be thoughtfully laid out in order to create the most value possible for your organization. Others may feel like your teams are going through the motions. Practices must be intentionally designed to create the most value possible. We recommend listing all of the practices in your organization and rating them high, medium, or low for the value you believe they are creating.

Then ask the question: *What can we do to improve the return on these practices?*

Practices must be intentionally designed to create the most value possible.

Evaluating your existing practices through the lens of creating the most value possible reveals opportunities to improve the return on these practices. What would be different in your organization if all meetings created high value over the collective value they create today? The MIND Methodology forces low-return practices to the surface to be addressed. Comparatively, every practice in the MIND Methodology is designed to create the most value and continually increase that value over time.

How would you rate the effectiveness of meetings in your organization?

Biggest Takeaways from Chapter Five

- There should be a strong connection between an intentional culture in your organization and its financial performance and impact.
- Culture is made up of the beliefs, accountability, practices, and decisions from which your organization creates value.
- Your alignment tools should promote behaviors creating the most value in your organization.
- Your alignment tools should also address non-value-creating behaviors as a developmental management tool.
- Functions within your organization can have very different cultures and subcultures.
- Be intentional about how you drive culture within your organization.

6

One Size Doesn't Fit All

Connect Leadership Development
to Financial Results

When speaking with those responsible for leadership development within their organization, most say they are very satisfied with the results. It doesn't matter how big or small the organization is. We've found this to be true in organizations ranging from 25 employees to 50,000 employees. Such people measure the effectiveness of a leadership development program based on satisfaction surveys sent to participants.

We always ask two revealing questions when we start a new client engagement:

1. How are you measuring the *impact* of your leadership development programs?
2. Are your leaders' Most Important Numbers improving as a result of their participation?

The most common response we hear is, "We can't measure that."

Everything your organization does should be performed with the intent of making it measurably better. Then the better measure of effective leadership development is in how it directly leads to improving a leader's results. Leaders must embrace and embody this mindset: "I need to perform now and get even better results tomorrow."

Everybody is at a unique stage in their leadership capability journey. This chapter shows you how to effectively and objectively evaluate a leader's capability and, more importantly, where to develop each leader next in order to create the most value for your organization.

A Surgical Approach to Leadership Development

One-size-fits-all leadership development programs don't make sense to me because each leader's development needs will differ due to their unique circumstances in matching their current capability with their specific, current business challenges. The MIND Methodology makes it easy to see exactly where a leader needs to develop next based on their performance to their Most Important Number. If you're consistently performing below your fore-casted MIN, you'll discover why by digging into your Drivers, Action Items, and the overall effectiveness of your meetings.

Applying a surgical approach to leadership devel-opment yields results quickly. If you're consistently achieving your MIN Forecast, the next question is simple but pointed:

What leadership capability do I need to improve upon to significantly increase the rate at which my team's MIN improves?

This level of ongoing introspection is how we rec-ommend leaders focus on their development at any time on the leadership development journey.

Every leader has blind spots. It's helpful to have an initial baseline capability conversation to help a leader to discover this and, as a result of the discovery process, be more open to learning and growing as a leader. The baseline leadership capability conversa-tion takes place between a manager and their direct report.

If you're the CEO and you lack a robust board of directors or a peer adviser you're comfortable with, we recommend reaching out to a MIND Methodology Certified™ Facilitator for these initial assessments and conversations. This ensures deep discovery is taking place. After a few of these assessments, it is easy for most leaders to become effective at facilitat-ing them.

MIND Leadership Competencies

We've identified six leadership competencies that represent a foundational capability for leaders. Each competency has specific abilities and behaviors associated with it. The six leadership competencies are as follows:

1. **Creating value**—Create value with all actions and decisions.
2. **Making decisions**—Accelerate value creation intentionally.
3. **Executing strategy**—Connect the dots between strategy, execution, and culture.
4. **Building capability**—Build infrastructure and people to achieve your MIN.
5. **Strengthening Leadership**—Eat and dream at the same time, creating an energizing environment for those around you.
6. **Shaping strategy**—Analyze and balance the elements required to compete for profits.

Depending upon a leader's level of hierarchy within an organization, the assessment conversation can take anywhere from ninety minutes to multiple hours to complete over a few sessions. Leadership levels include frontline leads, mid-level managers, senior managers, and executive-level leaders. While multiple hours may seem like a long time, it is an investment in future performance.

The dialogue surrounding each competency will differ based upon leadership level. Shaping strategy, for example, is quite different for a frontline leader than for a CEO.

For the frontline leader, it might be as simple as providing ideas to accelerate the value their team creates once implemented. Shaping strategy for the CEO will be reflected in their ability to create a comprehensive plan to clearly outline where the organization is currently, where it's going, and how to get there.

Prior to starting the competency discussion, most leaders say they understand what each competency means, and they are generally doing well, or really well, at applying it. When you start digging by asking for measurable examples when applying the associated abilities and behaviors for each competency, however, you can quickly assess a leader's true capability level.

Just because a leader lacks capability within a certain competency, it doesn't automatically mean it is where they need to develop next. The most effective leadership development work has to be focused on where each leader can create the most value for the organization *and* themselves.

Case Study: Customized Leadership Development

I am currently engaged in leadership development coaching for the Chief Operating Officer (COO) of a highly successful manufacturing business. The CEO requested my coaching to focus primarily on how the COO behaved in meetings, so he could learn to refrain from getting visibly frustrated. I was also tasked to help him communicate more effectively with team members by being more data driven and less emotionally driven.

The COO wanted me to focus on his ability to be a strong leader independent of the business. I asked both if it was okay for me to develop the COO to create value faster for the organization. Observing him do the work associated with improving the company's MIN, it was quickly apparent he needed to work on three things:

1. Earn the CEO's respect so he could successfully implement his ideas without being shot down. The COO had great ideas and was generally accurate with decisions and actions to improve the company's MIN, but he had difficulty communicating his plans in a way the CEO could support.

2. Intentionally develop his direct reports to accelerate value creation on their own. The COO was not intentional about developing his direct reports to improve their teams' MINs and accelerate value creation for the business.

3. Improve organizational structure and resource allocation.

There was no clear mapping of the organizational structure in order to be intentional about its design and continuous improvement. As covered in Chapter Three, the most productive way to approach this is to first decide on the outcomes you want to achieve, then design the ideal structure to achieve these outcomes (roles, responsibilities, allocation of resources, external resources) and match people to this structure based on their capabilities.

Case Study: Unpacking the Results

In the first seven months of leadership performance coaching, the company has increased sales and profits by over 50 percent. The COO began communicating and planning in a much more data-driven way. The CEO is satisfied with the progress and has given the COO more authority, autonomy, and decision rights. The COO's direct reports meet with him weekly for one hour with the sole purpose of developing each report to continually improve how they *eat and dream at the same time*.

During these meetings, he covers the performance of their MINs, works through critical decisions that need to be made and obstacles to value creation, and confirms how they are developing their direct reports and their specific development areas. The COO has also designed the ideal structure for the organization, and after fifteen months, the company was seeing four times the average monthly net profit over where this leadership engagement started.

The MIND Methodology makes it easy to observe and specify what skills and behaviors a leader currently needs to develop to create the most value for the organization. Think of it as a continuous retrospective process where you have identified the desired

MIN, then remain in a position to observe the actual, measurable results over time to recognize real-time leadership development adjustments to maximize your results. Let's explore how the six leadership competencies noted above allow leaders to effectively manage using the right MINDset.

1. Creating value—Create value with all actions and decisions.

Everything your organization does should be aligned to continually creating more value—for your employees, customers, and stakeholders. Winning organizations iterate faster and smarter by creating more value than their competition. Aligning all team members to value creation significantly increases your chances of being successful in any economic condition. The goal is to create so much value for your customers that they request even more of your products and services in bad times. This is *not* a typical mindset for most leaders.

The MIND Methodology works to ingrain this way of thinking in all leaders and non-supervisory team members. Possessing a value-creation MINDset is perhaps *the most important* foundational leadership perspective to have.

It can be very revealing to ask your leaders the following two questions:

1. How do you create value for our organization?
2. How does your team create value for our organization?

Typically, leaders respond with descriptions of their activities or those of their team members. Doing activities well and working hard doesn't always equate to measurable increases in value.

We've all heard the saying, "Don't confuse efforts with results." It's more powerful to hear a leader say they create value for the organization by continually improving their team's Most Important Number. Further, they can passionately show you how their team's Drivers, Action Items, KPIs, and MIND Meetings improve their MIN.

2. Making decisions—Accelerate value creation intentionally.

When, where, and how a leader makes critical decisions significantly impacts value creation for their teams and overall organizational performance. Critical decisions are relative to the MIN impact for each team. A decision at the senior leadership team level to increase cash flow by 10 percent will certainly create more overall value for the organization. At the functional level, the shipping team's critical decision might be to modify the flow of their process to allow them to ship 10 percent more packages without adding any additional labor hours.

Both are critical decisions relative to the value each team was designed to create. Making relatively few effective critical decisions has the potential to create significantly more value than any other practice. To ensure you are making critical decisions with the right MINDset, ask yourself, "What critical decisions do I need to make *today* to create the most value for our organization?" Distinguishing between critical and noncritical decisions is contingent upon improving the MIN.

In some cases, critical decisions are designed to prevent the MIN from going backward. An example of this could be a decision to implement a quality management system where there isn't one. It will add cost and may not directly improve an organization's profit MIN (although it can), but it can minimize the risk of a major product or service quality issue that could significantly hurt the organization's profit MIN.

As a leader, it's important to remember a big part of your job is making decisions to continually increase the value your team creates over time. It is helpful to keep an up-to-date list of decisions to positively impact your MIN and then appropriately act on them when the timing is right.

This MIN-improving, decision-making process can be as simple as collecting the right amount of information, assessing possible risks, selecting the best course of action, and then monitoring the MIN impact. Continuously monitoring the impact of a decision is important so you can quickly course correct if needed.

3. Executing strategy—Connect the dots between strategy, execution, and culture.

Executing strategy addresses a leader's ability to systematically implement MIN-based initiatives into action. It requires leaders to create MINs, Drivers, and

Action Items for all team members to be fully aligned with the organization's strategy. All functions, teams, and team members should know the role they play in executing on the organization's strategy. If they don't, it will be nearly impossible to fully execute.

Many leaders tend to hold back on sharing strategy information with a large percentage of the team members. Not doing so will significantly limit their ability to make the best value-creating decisions. Besides, doing the work of improving what is most important is not a *set-it-and-forget-it* process. There is no end—or limit—to how much a team can improve the value they create for the organization or how well they execute on strategy.

The longer a team does the work of improving what is most important using the MIND Methodology, the better they will get at executing on strategy. Leaders should be intentional about reviewing strategy elements applicable to their team and distilling out the MINs, Drivers, and Actions to achieve these elements.

4. Building capability—Build infrastructure and people to achieve your MIN.

Building capability covers many things, including the capacity of your facilities' output, the bandwidth of your people, processes, systems, equipment, intellectual property, and acquiring competitors. It's important to know how a leader thinks about the value of building capability and how adept they are at building different aspects of it as the company grows.

Do you know the right capabilities to have in order to create the most value for your business? Identifying the right areas to build on your current capabilities will always be somewhat of a moving target. Two months ago, it could have been sales needed to increase the capability to hit sales targets to achieve the company MIN. Today, it may be production. In two months, it may be product development. Simultaneously, there is likely a continuous need to build and develop the capability of your team members to think and act more productively.

It's important to always consider which capabilities need to be enhanced or added over the next twelve to thirty-six months in order to have the most positive impact on your MIN. The capability bottlenecks are ever-evolving, so building capability in the right order and at the right time is critical to reach your organization's desired outcomes and achieve your MIN.

5. Strengthening Leadership—Eat and dream at the same time, creating an energizing environment for those around you.

As previously mentioned, eating means leaders getting results now, and dreaming refers to developing capability and making decisions to get better results in the future.

This competency addresses the abilities and behaviors at each level of leadership to cause extraordinary results to happen within your organization. How a leader is perceived by team members and other coworkers, as well as the consistency and predictability of their behaviors, creates the environment for their teams to produce. This is the difference between unleashing positive, productive energy intrinsically from a team or throttling it.

After performing a MIND Baseline Leadership Assessment with a leader, we find many don't intentionally think about their role in this way. With all of the leadership development content and materials currently available, there seems to be a significant lack of self-awareness in this area. We have found this to be a common area for improvement for many leaders.

A leader's primary job is to create an energizing environment for team members, unleashing positive, productive energy. This includes being supportive and developmental with every team member, removing obstacles, providing relevant resources, and setting clear rules of engagement to encourage the right behaviors to accelerate improvement in the MIN.

6. Shaping strategy—Analyze and balance the elements required to compete for profits.

Many organizations have limited resources yet infinite possibilities for solutions to add value to their organization and stakeholders. When creating and shaping strategy, leaders need to be able to effectively work with what they have to deliver the next-level results they are shooting for. As results improve, so will the availability of resources to achieve even greater results.

This concept is cyclical in nature. Leaders seem to be in one of two camps when it comes to how they view their available resources to accomplish their strategy.

- First Camp—These leaders see a lack of resources. This is their default response for not being able to achieve an identified desired result. When in this camp, it doesn't seem to matter if their annual budget is $700,000, $7 million, or $7 billion. There is never enough.

- Second Camp—It doesn't matter what resources the leader has to work with. They are excited for whatever resources they have. Oftentimes, their resources aren't even financial. They constantly leverage what they currently have to work with to achieve better results.

When assessing a leader around creating and shaping strategy, the most important thing is their mindset around identifying and leveraging available resources. There is always a better way, and it is the leader's job to find it!

Biggest Takeaways from Chapter Six

- One-size-fits-all leadership development programs rarely deliver the results you are looking for.
- Make sure your leaders are doing the right amount of *eating* and *dreaming*.

- Surgically develop leaders where they can create the most value at any point in time.
- Leaders often need to be developed in both how they show up and their capability.
- Develop leaders through the lens of accelerating value creation.

7

Performance Snapshots™ Your Teams Will Love

Everyone Needs to Know What's Expected and Where They Stand 100 Percent of the Time

How much fun is it to try putting together a jigsaw puzzle without having the box to show what the final puzzle is supposed to look like?

No, thank you.

This is the same feeling most employees have regarding their annual performance review. Most enter the meeting with anxiety and leave in anger.

Imagine the opposite—a world where you enter your performance review with clarity and leave enthusiastic about what's ahead. This world does exist, and it's a common experience within the MIND Methodology.

Performance Reviews People Love

It is rare to find leaders, or any team members, who will say they love the performance reviews. One client told me she breaks out in hives the night before giving a performance review to her team members because of the stress it causes. With performance reviews being so universally disliked, why do most managers continue doing them when the process feels so bad for everyone involved?

Even with the best of intentions, performance reviews usually turn into a check-the-box process, resulting in minimal impact on creating more value for the organization. Every employee should know what is expected and where they stand. Lack of clarity around individual and team performance expectations is the core reason most review processes do not provide the energizing, value-creating experience they should.

There is a better way!

This chapter introduces you to the MIND Methodology's Performance Snapshot Process. Eighty percent of the employees who experience the "MIND Performance Snapshot™" say they love it. The other 20 percent say our process is better than any performance review they have previously experienced. We have found even the most jaded employees leave the Performance Snapshot in a better state of mind.

Being clear about performance expectations is easy to say but challenging to sustain or do consistently across a variety of functions. It can be easy to assess a salesperson against a numerical revenue or conversion number, but what is the number you would measure a staff accountant against? And how do you evaluate any leader or team member to the application of the organization's mission, vision, values, or culture? Or how do you measure and evaluate how leaders and team members relate with others or in specific scenarios?

As you have probably figured out by now, when using the MIND Methodology, all aspects of the business are tied in some way, shape, or form to value creation. Whether it's performance management, human resource or talent management, culture work, engagement initiatives, training initiatives, or quality initiatives, the outcomes need to point to improving the MIN.

Performance Snapshots are designed to be an energizing process providing clarity around what is expected and how well each team member is meeting expectations 100 percent of the time.

Performance Snapshot Criteria

With few exceptions, the Performance Snapshot is designed so each team member has three areas that rarely change unless the employee changes roles. These areas include:

1. **The team's MIN performance**—The team's MIN evolves and is reforecast over time in order to continually create more value.
2. **The employee's outcome-based responsibilities**—Responsibilities may occasionally be refined as the role evolves.
3. **The culture**—The cultural "fit" and ability to apply culture is the same for every team member.

Performance Snapshots prevent surprises when it comes to performance and culture. When using the MIND Methodology, every team member should have a meeting with their manager at the right frequency to work on their personal and professional development and to ensure they know what is expected and where they stand 100 percent of the time.

Performance Snapshots are given with the other team members present and actively participating. For each of the three goals noted above, it's important to fully capture what each team member does well and where there are opportunities to improve. We find it almost impossible for one manager to see and remember every detail of a direct report's performance or behaviors. Feedback from the entire team provides a 360-degree view where little is missed and observations can be confirmed.

All feedback is captured live during the Performance Snapshot Process. The feedback builds on itself during the discussion as conversation tends to jog the memory of other team members. This process puts every team member in a supportive and developmental state. In conducting Performance Snapshots, each team member knows the strengths and areas for improvement of the other team members. This makes it easier for team members being evaluated to know who to reach out to for help and who they might be able to assist in developing.

While this may sound like a version of 360 reviews, traditional 360 assessments tend to not provide the intended value for a few reasons:

1. The process is too time intensive.
2. It takes too much discipline to sustain.
3. Information isn't leveraged properly.

As a result, most team members don't benefit from the process. The Performance Snapshot is the complete opposite. It can easily be worked into regular team meetings, and there are three reasons why it's preferred:

1. It takes about twenty minutes per team member.
2. These snapshots provide clarity about what to work on for the next six months.
3. It energizes other team members to support one another's development along the journey.

The perspective anytime you apply the MIND Methodology is the following: "How will this improve our Most Important Number?" The Performance Snapshot Process is no exception. You should always be thinking about how your feedback will help each team member develop in a way to improve the team's MIN even faster. This will also create more value for the person being evaluated.

One of your team member's biggest perceived weaknesses may not be the area of development to create the most value for the organization. The most value could be developing that person to build on a strength. In short, you can easily list dozens of things for a team member to work on improving, but there will always be just a few of those things to create far more value than all others on the list.

For example, it is very common for a leader to hit the "easy button" and say they would like to develop their own leadership capability. Most will read a book or enroll in a general leadership course. There may be some interesting concepts to explore, but this is not likely what the leader needs most when it comes to improving their team's MIN.

Team MIN Performance

Feedback during the Performance Snapshot should always be focused on where the team member should develop next in order to create the most value given their role in the organization.

One of the best things about the Performance Snapshot Process is it takes very little time to prepare because each goal is measured on a five-point scale. Let's walk through how they work. When a team meets, they select the team member they want to do a Performance Snapshot with and begin the process by reviewing the team member's MIN goal. Since this is a team goal (with few exceptions), the score will be the same for all respective team members.

Per the MIND Methodology, there are clear and objective criteria for determining the score. If the MIN is a revenue goal, the scoring criteria could be:

- Greater than 10 percent above plan scores a five.
- Greater than 5 percent to 10 percent above plan scores a four.
- Within 5 percent above or below plan scores a three.
- Greater than 5 percent to 10 percent below plan scores a two.
- Greater than 10 percent below plan scores a one.

The percentages for the scoring criteria should always be determined and agreed upon by the team. It is very important for it to be *their* agreed-upon MIN goal and *their* work the team developed to achieve the MIN. Once the MIN goal is objectively scored, the team shares what the team member does well when working to achieve the MIN and where there are opportunities to improve.

This is always a supportive and developmental conversation with much more of a complete picture of a team member's actions and behaviors than it would be with only one person facilitating a performance review.

Outcome-Based Responsibilities

Next, we move to the team member's set of outcome-based responsibilities. As discussed in Chapter Three, every team member will have clear, outcome-based responsibilities for their role. It's not uncommon for team members to perform the functions of more than one role, but generally, there will be one primary role.

It's important to note when using the MIND Methodology, we build outcome-based responsibilities rather than the prevalent job description lists. Job descriptions typically list activities or tasks an employee will be required to perform. In contrast, outcome-based responsibilities measure objective outcomes that an employee will be responsible for achieving. Outcomes are more directly related to adding value than tasks.

When building this out for a specific role within your organization, start with a set of two to four powerful outcome-based responsibilities. When you read them, you should know immediately whether or not the team member is *delivering* on them.

Example 1—President of a medium-sized consulting and services client:

- Meet or beat top-level forecasted MIN.
- Continually strengthen agreed-upon culture elements, and objectively connect culture to financial results.

- Ensure an ideal structure is in place to achieve our growth and profit projections.

For each of these outcome-based responsibilities, it's easy to assess how well the leader is delivering on them. This example reflects outcome-based responsibilities at the top leadership level within a business.

Example 2—Frontline shipping lead working in a warehouse:

- Ensure proper levels of inventory of shipping supplies to meet demand.
- Accurate fulfillment: Correct product and quantities in every box we ship.
- Refine shipping department layout as necessary to keep up with growth.

The scoring criteria to measure a team member's performance on how well they delivered on their two to four outcome-based responsibilities:

- Significantly exceeds expectations scores a five.
- Exceeds expectations scores a four.
- Meets expectations scores a three.
- Below expectations scores a two.
- Significantly below expectations scores a one.

During the Performance Snapshot activity, all team members will provide feedback regarding what the team member does well when delivering on their outcome-based responsibilities and where there are opportunities for improvement. After this supportive and developmental discussion, it becomes relatively easy to score the individual on their specific role's responsibilities goal.

Tying Culture to Performance

Once this is completed, we move on to the team member's culture goal. The process is the same as above, but the scoring criteria are different. For a team member to live the company's culture in a way to accelerate value creation, they need to know how to properly apply the company's agreed-upon alignment tools—the foundation for driving an intentional culture.

Properly applying alignment tools means each team member can articulate or demonstrate an experience when they exhibited one or more of the agreed-upon alignment tools. Demonstrating these behaviors creates more value for the employee, the company, and your customers. As a brief reminder, these alignment tools can include your mission, set of values or behaviors, purpose statement, and vision statement.

The scoring criteria to assess an individual's proficiency with the organization's alignment tools connecting culture to financial results:

- Are you a cultural fit: "No" scores one point. "Yes" scores two points.

- Are you intentionally living our alignment tools to the benefit of our internal and external stakeholders? If not, add zero points. If yes, add one or two points depending on how well (Can you articulate an example of how you demonstrated this in the past six months?).
- Are you intentionally influencing other team members to "live" our alignment tools to create more value for the company? If not, add zero points. If yes, add one point. Must have examples.

Discussion: Which alignment tools do you live out well, and which alignment tools offer opportunities for development?

Obviously, if the team member isn't a cultural fit, you should be having another conversation. It's important for every team member to work in an environment where they are a cultural fit so they can thrive. On the few occasions where you have a team member who isn't a cultural fit, I believe it's our leadership responsibility to develop them to make it work within our intentional culture or help them find a better fit somewhere else. Everyone will be happier when we get this right.

It's an entirely different way of looking at culture when teams are discussing how each member is applying a particular value such as "integrity" to accelerate value creation. Most culture discussions are more along the lines of feel-good discussions. Time after time, I've seen these culture discussions within the Performance Snapshot Process have a supercharging effect on driving and strengthening culture within any organization.

I recently met with a consultant who has been working with one of our middle market clients for ten years on culture, based on a book titled, *The Collaborative Way*. We began working with this client as well and implemented the MIND Methodology over an eighteen-month time frame. The consultant told us he'd never seen such an improvement in culture in one year by simply using the MIND Methodology to drive it. He further said the MIND Methodology pours rocket fuel on their process!

The most important element when reviewing a team member's performance is to create alignment with the rest of the team in doing the right work in the right order at the right time to improve the team's MIN. This lens needs to drive every aspect of the performance improvement and professional development discussion.

Ideally, I believe performance and desired behaviors should be tied to compensation. How the two connect needs to be clear and easy to understand by every team member going through a Performance Snapshot. If not, this lack of clarity will create tension and take away from the discussion on how to contribute to creating more value as a contributing team member.

Scoring criteria can be either too vague or overly detailed in an attempt to cover every scenario. The vaguer the criteria, the more they are subject to widely varying interpretations. When this happens, the interpretation discussion takes precedence over the value-creation discussion. When criteria are overly detailed in a best-of-intentioned attempt to cover every scenario, it becomes too complicated and requires too much discipline to sustain over time.

Whether you implement the MIND Performance Snapshots or have another type of performance review, it is important to achieve these three things:

1. It is objective and very easy to understand by any team member being evaluated, their manager, and the team members participating.
2. There is no question about how a team member's performance and behaviors affect their compensation.
3. It supports the conditions for driving performance and personal development discussions focused on creating more value for the team member, the company, its customers and stakeholders.

Doing the work in an intentional way to create the most value is more important than any software tool by itself. When a methodology works for your company as measured by the value it creates, we owe it to our team members to provide tools to make it easy to sustain and scale the proven methodology.

Too many times, I've seen companies sold on expensive performance management software, thinking it will solve their performance management challenge. Because they didn't develop a performance management methodology first, it is no wonder their performance management process is not much more than a ritual.

The MIND Performance Snapshot Process™ (MIND PSP)

The MIND Performance Snapshot Process can give a few senior leaders pause when initially considering it. This can be because some leaders are worried about how the poor performance discussion will be received by the individual and the team. This process isn't designed to pounce on poor performance. It is designed to develop and position everyone on the team to continually create more value over time.

It's not uncommon for a team member to be in the "wrong seat" for a long time. Sometimes, leaders move people into a position thinking the person will be great at it, even if they have no experience in it. The leader may believe he or she can train the person up for the new role because of great performance in a different position.

I've also seen leaders assign a number of different roles to one person. If the person is historically a high performer, the person is less likely to reach out for help when they cannot keep up with their new position or roles. In essence, we unwittingly set the person up for failure. Because leadership put someone in the wrong seat, it will limit team performance and can also create tension among team members.

When one person on the team isn't carrying their weight for long enough, it can negatively affect the team's culture. The best way to address this is to be direct, own our part of what isn't working, and work to resolve the issue. The MIND Performance Snapshot Process works extremely well in terms of identifying team members in the wrong roles and helping get them to a place where they can create the most possible value for the organization.

Recently, we were setting up the Performance Snapshot Process with the senior leadership team of a new client. The CEO asked me to come in one hour before the meeting to discuss a concern. He was worried about how the process would go with the Director of Engineering. He explained the engineering team's results had been well below expectations, and it had created significant tension within the senior team. He was worried the discussion would be heated and contentious. I encouraged the CEO to trust the process.

During the Snapshot, the director of engineering said he loved doing research and new product development work but had never enjoyed leading the team. He expressed he wasn't skilled at leading meetings and organizing work for the engineering team. The outcome of his Performance Snapshot was an agreement to appoint someone else as the director of engineering and focus his attention solely on new product development.

The conversation was productive and added a ton of positive energy to the team around the engineering challenges. Afterward, the now "former" director of engineering commented the process went way better than expected. He felt relieved and said he would be happier in his new role. The CEO immediately approved implementing the MIND Methodology Performance Snapshot Process for all team members, all the way to the frontline.

This process is an effective way to create the conditions whereby every team member knows what is expected of them. It allows them to know where they stand with respect to their performance and how they are perceived by other team members as it relates to the company's culture. Not getting this right can significantly throttle productive energy in your organization.

Think about your own organization. How much productive energy is being throttled by team members not fully knowing what is expected and where they stand? If you got this right, would your team create 10 percent more value in the next year? What about 20 percent or more?

Every practice in your organization should be designed to accelerate value creation and improve productive energy within the team. Most leaders do not approach designing organizational practices with these two things in mind. The good news is that it's never too late. Start implementing Performance Snapshot reviews today.

Biggest Takeaways from Chapter Seven

- Every team member should know what is expected and where they stand on performance 100 percent of the time.
- Each employee should be evaluated based upon three goals: team MIN, outcome-based responsibilities, and culture.
- Performance Snapshots should be team based to capture all the feedback.
- Performance Snapshots are designed to develop every team member to continually create more value over time.
- Performance Snapshots take little to no time to prepare for when teams are following the MIND Methodology.
- Be clear about where each team member should focus their efforts and development moving forward.

Conclusion:
Your Next Best Step

The other day I was explaining the MIND Methodology to a friend. He's a CEO and a student of many different business operating systems. He runs an international company, has a couple of decades of experience, and earned a doctorate in leadership.

He's newer to the concept, and he thinks in word pictures. I could see his lights turning on when he started to understand the model.

"I love your methodology because it's so simple," he said enthusiastically. He went on to tell me how so many businesses get overwhelmed by all the numbers. "It's like pilots in a cockpit. Have you ever seen how many dials, gadgets, and numbers are in front of their faces?"

I saw where his mind was going. "So what's the Most Important Number for a pilot?"

"I don't know," he said. "I'm sure there are many."

"True," I said. "But what's the Most Important Number. What's their MIN?" After a few more moments of silence, I provided the answer: "to land safely with all the passengers."

"That's it!" he replied. "Arriving on time or making sure everyone gets a beverage or anything else matters, but not compared to that Most Important Number."

I smiled. I knew he got it. And I also knew he'd never forget it. So many business operating systems overwhelm leadership, management, and employees because they're too complex to maintain. Continuing the plane metaphor, imagine certain team members measuring success by how many peanuts they've distributed. Other team members measure success based on the number of airplane credit card applications completed during the flight.

You can pass out all the peanuts and collect fifty credit card applications, but if a passenger dies during the flight, then that team missed the mark.

So what about you? Is your Most Important Number clear? If not, we've included a self-implementation guide in the Appendix. It's customizable for you and your team.

Or, if you want some help, our team is ready, willing, and able. In fact, our passion and purpose are leading teams to discover and improve their Most Important Numbers.

We've included a couple of next steps below. It's time to increase productive collaboration, achieve your strategy, and execute to win.

Step 1: Introduce the MIND Methodology to your senior team.

Step 2: Have them read *Your Most Important Number*.

Step 3: Discuss with your senior team what would be different with this approach to creating more value as an organization.

Step 4: Make a decision on implementing the MIND Methodology.

Step 5: If the decision is yes, make a decision on doing it yourself (DIY) or finding a MIND Methodology Certified Facilitator at TheMindMethodology.com. These experienced individuals will facilitate the implementation of the MIND Methodology, starting with your senior leadership team.

Appendix: The DIY Approach to the MIND Methodology™

The MIND Methodology "How To" Guide

We recommend using a MIND Methodology Certified Facilitator to integrate the MIND Methodology within your organization. This is the most effective and efficient approach. Some teams, however, are unable to leverage a MIND Certified Facilitator. For this reason, we've created a DIY approach as well.

This Appendix provides practical, straightforward guidelines for your leadership and team members to instill the MIND Methodology foundation and processes in as much (or as little) of your organization you choose.

The key is ensuring you get the "MINDset" of the MIND Methodology in place. This includes the basics of *how teams do the work of improving what is most important*, starting with the senior leadership team. Be super curious about what decisions and actions you can take today to create the most short-term value and the most "net" long-term value.

Circling back to the Introduction, we believe a superstar leader can make just about any operating system work. The danger in this scenario, however, is that when the superstar leaves, the operating system does too. Complex operating systems don't transfer well. Complexity prevents scalability. This is why we prefer the MIND Methodology. Every team member can understand and implement their Most Important Number. By keeping it simple, everybody buys into the process. Simplicity ensures scalability.

Many operating systems say you will need strong leadership in place before it works. The MIND Methodology quickly builds the leadership from its current state. The development of strong, effective leadership is a by-product of the MIND Methodology.

Start Where You Are

Step one is the recognition that all team members can work to improve the MIN through everything they do. Once this MINDset is instilled in your team, step two is making sure your team is doing the right work in the right order at the right time. An easy way to think about this is ensuring your team is continually improving the perceived and actual value of your product or service. This should be unending, *evergreen* work.

Once you're getting traction with customers buying your product or service, the MIND Methodology ensures all team members have an ongoing focus to continually improve its value. Doing the right work in the right order at the right time is the quickest way to scale it. As we've mentioned earlier in this book, too many companies work on scaling before they have something to scale. Making this mistake wastes valuable time and money regardless of the organization's stage or life cycle of products and services.

If you're a startup or early-stage company, the MIND Methodology will ensure your team is focused on solving for product-market fit, as this is what is most important before moving on to scaling. At this stage, you're looking for objective scalable traction, not just positive feedback or reactive excitement. It's an easy trap for founders to get caught up in the thinking: "Everyone loves our idea—therefore, we've made it, and the only thing left to do is raise money and hire people."

This is a mistake. First, you must discover your **proven** product or service and provide scalable traction.

To do this, you must do a deep dive into unpacking the problem you set out to solve. Beyond excitement, you must be up-to-date in creating the change in value for your customers. You need to create enough customer perceived value for them to want to choose your product or service.

Ask yourself, "Would I switch to our product or service over our best competitor?" And, if so, *why*? If you don't have compelling answers resonating with your customer base, then keep improving your customers' perceived value of your product or service until you do.

The Rollout Process

The order in which you roll out the MIND Methodology matters. For this to be most effective, you have to start at the top of your organization and cascade out to your functional teams. You might be a sole proprietor, or maybe you manage thousands of employees. With the exception of rolling the MIND Methodology out to more than the senior team, everything else here will apply to any circumstance, even if you're a sole proprietor.

Although the order in which you implement the MIND Methodology may change a bit depending on your business conditions, here is the implementation order we have found works for most organizations (with details for each section below):

1. Senior team
2. Structure
3. Second-level teams
4. Strategy
5. Intentional culture
6. Performance Snapshots

7. Continue cascading MIND Meetings to front-lines teams
8. Surgical leadership development
9. Year-over-year (YOY) accelerated value creation by deeper understanding and application

Let's unpack these one at a time.

1. Start with your senior leadership team.

Whether you're a sole proprietor or you have employees numbering in the tens of thousands, you need to first get aligned at the top. If not, you'll only scale confusion. Malalignment trickles all the way to the front line and out to your contractors.

Begin with the MIND Meeting for your senior leadership team to quickly improve alignment, decisions, and accountability. Alignment is organizing all of the ideas, observations, and wisdom into categories of work to improve your Most Important Number. As we've observed throughout the book, these categories of work are called Drivers.

Next, decide which Drivers you will work on at any point in time to create the most value for the organization today. From there, assign Action Items within your Drivers to measurably improve your MIN. Regularly assigning and following up on Action Items will quickly improve your culture of accountability.

The goals for the senior leadership team MIND Meeting are as follows:

Prior to the MIND Meeting:

- Check In updates (wins, critical information, and where you need help) are entered in the MIND Meeting agenda by all team members the day before the meeting.

- All team members review Check-In updates, MIN progress, and In Focus Drivers prior to the meeting to be fully prepared to productively participate. This usually takes fifteen to twenty minutes.

During the MIND Meeting:

- Identify and share wins from every team member to build a winning culture and leverage the positive energy within the team. Each team member states their win quickly and refrains from elaborating unless asked for more information. Each win should take less than one minute to cover. Wins should be shared by participants at every MIND Meeting.

- Build decision-making capability within each team member by having them share information the team should know in order to make better decisions (quickly share and do not let this take the meeting off track).

  o Each person should share this information for the first four meetings. After the fourth meeting, there is no reason to continue reading this information aloud at each meeting because everyone should have read it before the meeting. Only read aloud if there are unanswered questions about the information. Do not let this derail the meeting.

- Share where you need help (obstacles in your way or resources needed to create more value for the organization).

- Agree to a Most Important Number reflecting—above all other numbers—whether your team is winning or losing the game.

- Agree to a stretch, but realistic, forecast for your MIN to track if your team is ahead, on, or behind plan.

- Identify categories of work, or Drivers, the team can leverage to improve the MIN.

- Define what the ideal state is for each Driver, and assess how the team is currently leveraging each Driver today to improve the MIN.

- Decide which one to three Drivers the team will name "In Focus" at any point in time to have the biggest impact on improving the MIN.

- Assign Action Items within Drivers to specific team members with a due date to ensure the team is doing the right work in the right order at the right time.

- The senior leadership meeting is all about improving alignment, decisions, and accountability. All of the detailed work is done between the meetings. Keep the meeting on track by not letting it dive into fully solving or admiring problems. As the facilitator of the meeting, you must listen through the filter: "Does this conversation impact our MIN?"

- Always finish the MIND Meeting with the Biggest Takeaways. Each team member should state the one takeaway they believe will create the most value for the organization. This is designed to continually improve each team member's ability to think about and create value faster for the organization.

After the MIND Meeting:

- Facilitator: Review areas to improve the flow of the meeting in order to allow the team to do their best work improving what is most important. Incorporate these improvements in your next meeting. Sometimes, this requires coaching team members off-line to ensure they hit the ground running for the next meeting.
- All team members: Review and stay on top of all of your Action Items between meetings. Be prepared to come into the next MIND Meeting with a plan to proactively improve what is most important.

This meeting should take place weekly for eight weeks and tends to initially last approximately 90 to 120 minutes. Once the work is organized and aligned over the first three to four meetings, the meeting duration will quickly drop, and you will be amazed at how fast your team is improving alignment, decision-making, and evolving into a culture of accountability. After eight weekly meetings, you can set the right cadence going forward. Most clients are able to reduce their meeting duration to 60 minutes or less.

Most senior teams keep the weekly cadence but get a lot more done in much less time. MIND Meetings should only take as long as they need to. When your team is fully aligned, making good decisions, and has a strong culture of accountability, a thirty-minute meeting can be more than enough at times. It is normal, however, to take a few months to get there.

It will rarely take more than four to eight weeks to get your best work and opportunities organized and aligned using the MIND Methodology. If you find your team is struggling to organize and align, don't hesitate to reach out to a certified MIND Methodology Certified Facilitator for help.

Your Most Important Number & Driver meeting keeps the focus on what's most important

Figure A-1

Initially, identify the one person on your senior leadership team with the most effective facilitation skills and who will keep MIND Meetings on track (see Figure A-1). Having this person facilitate the first few meetings will speed up adoption and the quality of work the team is doing to improve what is most important. Within a few months, everyone on your team should be able to effectively facilitate your senior leadership team MIND Meetings.

It is key for everyone on your team to show up proactively prepared to improve your MIN. When you hold everyone accountable for being proactively prepared for these meetings, you will be amazed at how the quality of the work improves over time. The question I like to ask is, "Are we more aligned, making better decisions, and doing better work today than we were six months ago?" If the answer is yes, then you are on the right track. If the answer is no, then reevaluate how the team is doing the work of improving what is most important.

If you're a small startup or early-stage business with ten or fewer employees, keep going with the senior leadership team MIND Meetings to continue to improve your team's alignment, decision-making, and culture of accountability. At the appropriate time, you will want to incorporate structure, outcome-based responsibilities, and MIND Methodology Performance Snapshots. Guidelines will be addressed further in this chapter.

2. Structure

Organizational structure should be addressed within your first eight senior leadership team meetings, and most organizations make "structure" a Driver in the first set of Drivers created. Getting the structure right is a moving target for any growing organization. At this stage of deploying the MIND Methodology, you know what the Most Important Number is for your organization. Now you are asking the question, "Do we have the right structure to achieve the MIN?" As covered in Chapter Three, the proper order is outcomes, structure, then people.

Laying out the structure for the senior leadership team to review makes it easy to ask and address these questions:

- **Elements**: Do we have all of the functional elements necessary to achieve our MIN?
- **Resources**: Are we properly allocating resources across our structure to improve our MIN in the fastest and most effective way possible?
- **Leadership**: Are any of our leaders carrying too much load to be as effective as they could be?
- **Roles**: Do we have clearly defined roles, each with two to four outcome-based responsibilities within our structure?
- **Responsibility**: Does every leader assigned to a role within this structure have the capability to deliver on the role's outcome-based responsibilities?

- **Structure**: Which part of our structure is currently holding us back the most from achieving our MIN?

These are six powerful questions to ask while looking at your organization's functional structure. The goal of this exercise is to accelerate continuous growth in the value your organization creates over time as measured by improvements in your MIN. Review the simple, functional structure in the graphic below:

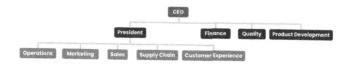

Figure A-2

Imagine asking and addressing the six questions above for each functional element of this structure example. Maybe the supply chain is currently holding the MIN back the most due to constantly running out of materials needed to deliver your products and services on time.

- What are all the roles identified within the supply chain function?
- Are the outcome-based responsibilities clearly defined for each role within the supply chain function, and are they the right deliverables?

- Have we allocated the right number of resources to the supply chain function?
- Do all team members within the supply chain have the capabilities to deliver on the outcomes required for each role?

It's important to note this process is based on functional capabilities and capacity. It's never personal. Rather, it's all about setting up every team member for success and creating value at an accelerated rate.

When you study your organizational structure and address these six questions, you may find you're missing a function or two required to achieve your MIN. As you grow, this will almost certainly happen. With this approach to leveraging organizational structure, you'll have the ability to be intentional and proactive about addressing structural bottlenecks long before they become major issues.

3. Second-Level Teams

If you have more than ten to twelve employees, your next action will be to eventually cascade the MIND Meetings to your senior leadership team member's functional teams (second-level functional teams). The objectives for these MIND Meetings are the same as they are for the senior leadership team. Examples of these types of teams can include sales, marketing, customer service, supply chain, and production.

Functional team MINs are typically different from the top-level MIN for the company (but not always) but when improved, will directly improve the overall company MIN. Mapping MINs and the work being done to improve them is a powerful way to ensure every team is pulling in the same direction.

Most Important Numbers (MINS) align your teams

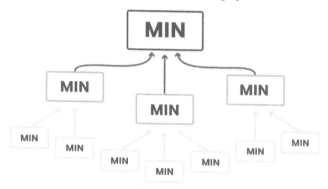

Figure A-3

As you start cascading the MIND Meetings to second-level teams, you will want to evaluate your organization's structure to ensure it supports your desired outcomes. This was detailed in Chapter Three. Being able to clearly see your organization's structure makes it easy to spot gaps or an imbalance in the allocation of resources.

At any point in time, there will be one part of this structure holding the organization back more than all of the others. It may be marketing not generating enough qualified leads or customer service not delivering the experience your customers expect. These organizational structure bottlenecks are a continuously moving target and should always be in focus by your organization's leaders.

Once second-level teams and beyond are practicing the MIND Methodology, we recommend the next activity is to facilitate cross-functional collaboration MIND Meetings. Schedule cross-functional meetings once it is clear the functional teams have an effective MINDset in their meetings. Cross-functional collaboration meetings should be made up of leaders from each team practicing the MIND Methodology.

The focus of these meetings is twofold:

- First, working as a group to help improve each other's MIN.
- Second, to address and eliminate the current organizational structure bottleneck.

The quality of the application of the MIND Methodology will vary from team to team. Having these team leaders work together to improve one another's MIN accelerates every team's ability to create value faster through better alignment, decision-making, and accountability.

Here's an example of an effective cross-functional collaboration meeting agenda:

- Review status of current organizational structure bottleneck:
  - What is the current status of their MIN?
  - What is the work being done to improve their MIN?
  - How can the other team leaders help to get their MIN back on track?
- Where do we think the next organizational structure bottleneck will be?
  - Why?
  - What are we doing to get in front of it?
- MIN review for non-bottleneck teams:
  - What is the current state of their MIN?
  - What meaningful work is being done to keep the MIN on or ahead of plan?

4. Strategy

At its core, strategy is answering three basic questions:

1. Where are we now?
2. Where are we going?
3. How will we get there?

Every organization is a little different in terms of how to address strategy, if at all. Those who recognize the value in developing a strategy generally participate in an annual strategy "retreat" or session but rarely spend the equivalent amount of time determining how to implement it.

Many leaders aren't clear regarding what their strategy session will need to address in order to create the most value for all stakeholders. At the end of the day, we know what they all have in common are the three questions listed above. Refer to Chapter Four for clear detail and guidance.

For DIY purposes, we recommend the following general guidelines for creating your strategy:

Prework for an effective strategy session:
- Distribute the following recommended survey questions to your leadership team one week before your strategy session (we recommend using a survey tool, such as SurveyMonkey®, Typeform®, or another polling-type application):
  o What is the big picture view of the markets we serve, and how will these conditions impact us in the short and long run?
  o What did our strongest competitors do in the last year to change the game, and how did it work out for them?
  o What did we do in the past year to change the game, how did it work out for us, and what could we have done better?
  o What keeps you up at night when you think about the future of our business?
  o What does aspirationally winning look like for this year?
  o What does aspirationally winning look like two to three years out?

- ○ What are the critical things we have to get done this year to aspirationally win this year and set us up to win bigger two to three years out?
- Ensure all leadership team members invest time to read all of the responses prior to the meeting in order to hit the ground running. This will allow the team to be fully prepared for discussion and will accelerate value creation from decisions derived during the session from these responses.

During the strategy session:
- Take five to ten minutes to capture each person's expectations for the session's outcomes.
- Agree on purpose and rules of engagement for the meeting.
- Discuss survey responses and capture meaningful actions and decisions to be made.
- Where your business is now: What are your current strengths, weaknesses, and impactful conditions?
- Where are you going? Discuss and capture what aspirationally winning looks like for the team.
- How are you going to get there? Identify (or confirm) your top-level MIN, Drivers, Action Items, KPIs, and timelines.
- List all critical goals to accomplish by quarter in order to win this year and set you up to win bigger two to three years out.

- Review your organization's functional structure: Do we have the right structure and allocation of resources to achieve our MIN?
- For all critical roles, do we have people in those seats who can deliver on their role's outcome-based responsibilities?
- Capture critical decisions made or those that need to be made.
- Review expectations to ensure they were met.
- Capture every participant's biggest takeaway from the strategy session they believe will create the most value for your organization.

Post-work for an effective strategy session:
- Incorporate all strategy elements into the appropriate MIND Methodology plans:
  - MIN forecasts: What is the value of your MIN today, and what do you expect the MIN value to be in the future?
  - Driver elements: Description refinements to what a ten-state looks like, actions, and the addition or modification of Drivers to accelerate value creation.
  - Critical strategic goals to accomplish by quarter.

Depending on a number of variables, such as time constraints, culture, and availability, your strategy session may take a half day, a full day, or up to three days. In planning the strategy session, I recommend you think deeply about what your team can do to accelerate the value they create. You may have to address culture or compensation strategy as well if this is an area you believe is materially impacting your MIN.

You may need to address leadership development and your people development practices in general. You have limited time and resources, so how will you plan for coming out the other side of your strategy session, ensuring full alignment to doing the right work in the right order at the right time? It is very helpful if you keep coming back to the three foundational strategy questions:

- Where are we now?
- Where are we going?
- How will we get there?

5. Intentional Culture

Culture is the X factor when it comes to unleashing productive energy. You can have an amazing operating methodology to align all team members to doing the right work and pulling in the same direction, but if they are not fully engaged, it will be reflected in the speed of your value-creation machine. The purpose of strengthening culture is to increase engagement and productive energy. This is easy to say, yet much harder to do.

In Chapter One, we explored overarching organizational alignment tools, including mission, vision, and behaviors to drive an intentional culture. Moving into

Chapter Five, we covered how to foundationally connect culture to financial results by assessing shared core beliefs, decision-making, practices, and accountability.

As previously mentioned, everything your organization does should be driven by the intent of making it measurably better, and everything else is a waste of time and resources. If you don't have a foundation for your overarching cultural alignment tools, I recommend developing a mission and set of behaviors to start with. From there, you may choose to develop a purpose statement, vision, and set of leadership traits. Your mission should be developed by your entire leadership team, and the behaviors should be developed with the input of *all team members* in your organization.

As a review, I recommend your mission be designed to tell customers in a compelling way why they should do business with you and, at the same time, tell all employees why they get a paycheck. If you don't deliver value for your customers, all jobs are in jeopardy. You will use your mission to align all employees to continually improve the value they create for your customers. Your set of behaviors should reflect the behaviors causing the best results to happen within your organization.

From a value-creation standpoint, they should cause 50 percent or more of your employees to behave, perform, and lead as good or better than the top 10 percent of performers at your strongest, most admired competitors. Get this right, and your competition won't have a chance.

Ensure your mission is thoughtful and something all employees can get behind. This is an alignment tool used to accelerate the value your organization creates, not a marketing slogan. Your set of behaviors will drive how all of your team members engage with one another to both support your mission and achieve your MIN Forecast over time.

If you want significant buy-in, it's very important to survey all employees for their input. Start by telling them what you want to accomplish by establishing a set of observable, desired behaviors. Then ask them for the winningest behaviors they have observed from others on their best days. From this list, you will be able to distill a set of four to six behaviors to drive an intentional, winning culture within your organization.

Although you can certainly facilitate this process within your own organization, it's often better to have an outside resource facilitate the process, as they are looking through a more objective lens. This is especially true if you have any symptoms of a toxic culture in any part of your organization. All organizations have a culture. In most organizations, this culture is not intentionally designed. It's far more powerful if your culture is intentional and drives the winning behaviors to achieve your Most Important Number.

6. Performance Snapshots

As previously detailed, every team member should know exactly what is expected and where they stand 100 percent of the time. Utilizing MIND Meetings across the organization, every participating team member should be clear about their team's MIN and the status of their respective Action Items to achieve their MIN.

There are two additional important elements for a team member to know exactly what is expected and where they stand 100 percent of the time. They include: 1) outcome-based responsibilities for each team member to own, and 2) how they "show up" (or are perceived by others) and how they interact with the team culturally. To effectively conduct Performance Snapshots, you will need to provide supportive and developmental feedback for each team member on the following three elements:

1. Their team's Most Important Number
2. Their set of two to four outcome-based responsibilities
3. Their application of your cultural alignment tools, as detailed in Chapter Five, to create value (core values, behaviors, mission, and vision)

For each team member, develop two to four outcome-based responsibilities. As covered in Chapter Seven, these outcome-based responsibilities should be clear, measurable, and allow you to easily assess whether or not a team member is doing well or not delivering on the value their role was designed to create.

Performance Snapshots are most effective when facilitated with the entire team an individual works with. For each of the three goals (team MIN, outcome-based responsibilities, and culture), encourage supportive and developmental feedback from the group around what the individual does well and where there may be current opportunities for improvement.

Once all of this is captured, make a succinct list of what the individual should focus on for the next six months with the intention of conducting Performance Snapshots biannually. I strongly recommend the individual being assessed and their manager both have access to the completed Performance Snapshot in order to discuss it in monthly one-to-one meetings for ongoing professional development purposes.

7. Continue Cascading MIND Meetings to Frontline Teams

As your senior leadership team gains confidence and traction with the MIND Methodology (which we have found to be around the sixth to eighth MIND Meeting), you may begin—as many of our clients do—to add additional teams into the fold through their own functionally based MIND Meetings. Cascading the MIND Methodology to your frontline teams can happen as quickly or as slowly as your culture allows.

As a general guideline, it's not uncommon for organizations with 100 to 500 employees to have all employees engaged in MIND Meetings within six months or less. The meeting formats may vary based on their *eating and dreaming* ratios (short- and long-term focus). On average, senior leadership teams should be spending 20 percent of their time eating (short-term results focus) and 80 percent of their time dreaming (doing things today to get a better result in the future).

Rolling out a MIND Meeting for any team follows the same process as for the senior leadership team. Team members generate their MIN and self-identify Drivers they can leverage to improve their MIN. They are also responsible for assigning Action Items to hold one another accountable for doing the work they have agreed to do: the right work in the right order at the right time. Each new team should have a well-versed MIND "champion" for one year to ensure the MIND Methodology is properly deployed within the new team.

The champion should be experienced in effectively facilitating MIND Meetings and a student of the MIND Methodology. How do we know if the champion is effective? The MIN should be improving. The MIND champion should fully facilitate the first eight weekly meetings, leaning in heavily for the first two meetings, then assisting another team member in facilitating the MIND Meetings by meeting number eight. Afterward, we recommend the MIND champion should attend one monthly meeting for the next ten months to further develop the team to leverage the MIND Methodology to improve their MIN.

8. Surgical Leadership Development

The MIND Methodology makes it easy to accelerate leadership development for any leader. Once a leader has several months under their belt running MIND

Meetings for their team, it is easy to see gaps in performance as well as opportunities to improve the MIN even faster. Leadership development will be in two areas. First, observe how they "show up" in terms of how their leadership energizes or de-energizes their team, and second, note their management capability and enough subject matter expertise to manage and facilitate strategy setting for the team.

As mentioned in Chapter Six, a one-size-fits-all leadership development program isn't nearly as effective as developing each leader exactly where they need it. With the MIND Methodology, it's easy to see one element of their performance by looking at the leader's team MIN. Performance is visible when using the MIND Meetings.

Drivers and actions taken to improve the MIN—as well as all the information the leader and their team are sharing in meetings to make better decisions—are visible. You can see within minutes if the leader is just checking boxes with their team or taking meaningful actions to really move the needle on their Most Important Number.

Observing a leader facilitating their team MIND Meetings and their one-to-ones with their direct reports will give you a good sense of how they are demonstrating their effectiveness as a leader. The best leaders we've observed exhibit positive energy in good times and especially bad times. They create an energizing environment for their team, and in return, get the highest levels of productive engagement from their team members.

Armed with information easily gleaned from following the MIND Methodology and observing the leader in action, you can create a list of developmental opportunities for each leader. Once you have this list, we recommend you prioritize it by developing the leader based on an assigned value to the organization and on each development opportunity. Then, simply tackle leadership development in the order of highest value or ROI to the organization. This, in turn, should create the highest value for the leader being developed as well.

9. Year-Over-Year Accelerated Value Creation by Deeper Understanding and Application

There is no end to how much your team or entire organization can improve alignment, decision-making, and accountability. The better you and your team get at doing the work, the faster you will be able to create value. It's important to be students of the MIND Methodology and live with the philosophy of there *always being a better way*—and it is your job to find it.

Accelerating value creation is never a *set-it-and-forget-it* endeavor. You know you're doing the right work when the MINs are improving. If they're not, then either the process has become more important than what's most important, or the team is not doing their best work of improving what is most important.

Some team members will say they're too busy doing work to do MIND Meeting "Check-Ins" or to participate in meetings. We have found these are usually the same people who, when assigned Action Items, have justifications for not getting them done on time. When we see this, we find it helpful to ask the question, "If not the MIND Methodology, what is your methodology for continually improving alignment, decision-making, and accountability?"

It's no surprise that when asked this question, they don't have a good answer. No matter what business operating system (intentional or unintentional) your organization agrees to use, it's more than reasonable to expect all team members to come in every day to create as much value as they can. They should also spend an appropriate amount of time finding better ways to create more value for customers, the organization, and the community in which it resides.

You may be wondering when the optimal time to start using the MIND Methodology might be. We've worked with hundreds of clients over the years and have found the best times to begin include when:

- You are in the early stages, or pre-revenue, and have not proven traction yet).
- Your business is experiencing growing pains.
- Your business is ripe for growth.
- Your business feels stagnant due to size, silos, or bureaucracy.
- Your business is significantly resistant to change.
- You recognize there isn't alignment among the senior leadership team.

- Your leadership team is undergoing changes or will be changing soon.
- You are planning an acquisition or sale.
- You are getting great results, but you know your business can do even better (unrealized potential).
- Your leadership team spends too much time putting out fires and feels stressed or overwhelmed.
- You have one or more big initiatives underway (and may not be getting the expected traction from your efforts).
- You are getting pressure from investors.

The best time to start is NOW!

When is it NOT the right time to improve alignment, decision-making, and accountability? It doesn't matter if your organization is on life support, getting solid results, or knocking it out of the park with incredible results—there is always a better way, and the MIND Methodology will help you and your team find it!

Bibliography

Carlucci, Ron. "How to Actually Encourage Employee Accountability." *Harvard Business Review.* November 23, 2020. https://hbr.org/2020/11/how-to-actually-encourage-employee-accountability.

Harter, Jim. "Historic Drop in Employee Engagement Follows Record Rise." *Gallup.* July 2, 2020. https://www.gallup.com/workplace/313313/historic-drop-employee-engagement-follows-record-rise.aspx.

O'Leary, Joel. "A One Degree Difference: The Compound Effect." *5AM JOEL.* February 6, 2020. https://5amjoel.com/one-degree-difference/.

Porter, Michael E. *Competitive Strategy: Techniques for Analyzing Industries and Competitors.* New York: Free Press, 1998.

Acknowledgments

This book is the culmination of decades of practical application of leadership lessons I've learned on the front lines within my businesses and hundreds of other organizations. There are too many individuals who contributed to my learning and development over the years to mention here. I would like to mention just a few.

I would like to thank Ali Parnian, president of ETW, for his tireless energy over the years running this *ultra-marathon* to develop the MIND Methodology. Thank you, my friend.

To Matt Glazier, you have led the development of our software technology from the early stages through today with a relentless pursuit of improving the MIND Methodology experience. We couldn't have done this without you. And I love that you and I share a wonderful passion for playing guitar.

I am thankful for the entire ETW team for their commitment to refining the MIND Methodology and relentlessly improving our clients' Most Important Numbers. You are a group of amazing people with whom I love working. Thank you for your hard work, sense of humor, and being all in on improving our Most Important Number.

To Jack Welch, thank you for taking me under your wing and being a trusted business partner. More than anything, thank you for being a caring, loving friend. I will always miss our conversations.

To the team at the Jack Welch Management Institute, thank you for the deep dive on leadership principles and exploring what works in the real world when it comes to delivering results.

To Ram Charan, thank you for helping me fully understand the power of connecting culture to financial results. You have been an incredible mentor, and words cannot fully express my gratitude.

To Rick Watts, John Jackson, Tony Mitteer and all the amazing team members at Able Aerospace, thank you for your friendship, candor, and hard work in building the business. The MIND Methodology would never have been developed without our collective experience.

To the thousands of leaders I have worked with in organizations ranging in size from one sole proprietor to tens of thousands of employees, this book could never have been written without your practical application of its principles.

Acknowledgments

To Cyndi Laurin and Kary Oberbrunner, thank you for your mentorship and guidance in writing this book.

To the MIND Methodology Certified Facilitators, thank you for your amazing work improving organizations using the MIND Methodology. I learn as much from your work as ours.

To Jessica Pacheco, thank you for the many hours of conversations around the concepts in this book. Your insights and mentorship on strategic thinking and clarity proved invaluable. Thank you, my love.

To Sofia and Eva Pacheco (aka, "The Pacheclets"), your energy makes the world a better place, especially mine!

About the Author

Lee Benson has accumulated more than 25 years of experience as a CEO, and he understands the challenges and tensions that come from putting people first while remaining focused on performance. After selling Able Aerospace for nine figures, he turned his attention to creating a system to help other leaders improve their company's results—the **M**ost **I**mportant **N**umber and **D**rivers, or MIND, Methodology. When implemented, MIND improves an organization's most important numbers as senior leadership teams develop an intentional, high-performance culture.

MINDset Assessment™

Discover Your Team Alignment Score™

Get clarity on how aligned you are
with value creation and making
critical decisions.

Assessment.YourMostImportantNumber.com

The MIND Methodology Community™

The Right Tools Make All the Difference

Get access to tools, exclusive content, and resources to help you improve Your Most Important Number.

Subscribe.YourMostImportantNumber.com

MIND Methodology Masterclass™

Leverage the MIND Methodology™ in your organization

Get exclusive training from expert facilitators to help you gain mastery in implementing the MIND Methodology.

Discover how to drive:

Alignment
Decisions
Accountability

Masterclass.YourMostImportantNumber.com

Find Your MIND Methodology Certified™ Facilitator

Improve Your Most Important Number Faster
Leverage the Proprietary Software to Scale Easier
Tap into Expert Insights and Experience

We're here to help

Facilitator.YourMostImportantNumber.com

The MIND Methodology
MasterMIND™

Expand Your Mindset.
Grow Your Leadership.
Strengthen Your Community.

Mastermind.YourMostImportantNumber.com

Bring the MIND Methodology™ to your audience

Invite Lee Benson to speak

He has a passion for helping companies
discover their Most Important Number.

**Increase Collaboration.
Achieve Your Strategy.
Execute to Win.**

Speaking.YourMostImportantNumber.com

BLOCKCHAIN
VERIFIED IP

Made in the USA
Las Vegas, NV
25 July 2022